DATE DUE

Integrating the Internet Into the Business Curriculum

National Business Education Association Yearbook, No. 36

1998

Editor:
Dennis LaBonty
Utah State University
Logan, Utah

Published by:
National Business Education Association
1914 Association Drive
Reston, VA 20191-1596
Tel: 703-860-8300 • Fax: 703-620-4483
Home Page: http://www.nbea.org/nbea.html • E-Mail: nbea@nbea.org

Integrating the Internet Into the Business Curriculum

Copyright © 1998 by the National Business Education Association

National Business Education Association
1914 Association Drive
Reston, VA 20191-1596

ISBN 0-933964-51-X

Any views or recommendations implied in this book do not necessarily constitute official policy of the National Business Education Association.

Two unrelated partners are influencing and shaping the business education curriculum. These partners are the Internet and the *National Standards for Business Education.*

The Internet is a remarkable resource of interconnected networks. Not since the microcomputer has a technology influenced the business education curriculum like the Internet. It is saturating every content area identified in the *National Standards for Business Education,* and it continues to exceed predictions about its impact on business, education, and society. Business educators at all levels are challenged to integrate Internet potential into their curricula through e-mail, online resources, business and educational Web sites, home page development, multimedia, "electronic" global travel, voice technology, and other applications.

The *National Standards for Business Education* has provided a solid curricular foundation involving 12 business content areas. "The primary purposes of this document are to provide the standard by which all business education programs are measured, to define anew the parameters of the discipline of business education as it has emerged in recent years, and to provide a document which curriculum writers can use as a guide in developing superior programs in business education." These Standards are positively influencing business education.

Information in the Yearbook looks at the Internet, the Internet related to selected National Standards content areas, and some visions by authors about the Internet and the business education profession. *Integrating the Internet Into the Business Curriculum* is divided into three parts.

Part I, *History and Policies,* addresses the Internet story and management policies. Administrative and management policies dealing with Internet use in the classroom are provided, including examples of Acceptable Use Policies and relevant administrative practices.

Part II, *Internet Applications Related to National Standards for Business Education,* deals with using the Internet in selected business education content areas. This section includes real and ideal examples of Internet uses and activities. Content areas include international business, personal finance, computer application courses, and others.

Part III, *Internet-Related Visions and Topics,* is a section about the Internet and its connections with the business education profession. This section looks at the Internet and its impact on the discipline of business and business teacher education.

I hope you will gain some new ideas or discover useful information from this Yearbook that will help you meet Internet challenges in the business curriculum. I would like to express my sincere thanks and appreciation to all those who contributed to this Yearbook. Special recognition goes to the chapter authors; the National Business Education Association's Publications Committee and NBEA publication staff; reviewers; and the department head and staff in the Department of Business Information Systems and Education at Utah State University.

Web site addresses listed in the chapters may have changed after the Yearbook was published. These addresses were accurate as of the writing of the chapters; however, their accuracy cannot be guaranteed over time.

Dennis LaBonty, Editor
Utah State University — Logan, Utah

contents

**Integrating the
Internet Into the
Business Curriculum**

Chapter 5

Jim Mansfield
University of Missouri-St. Louis — St. Louis, Missouri

Lonnie Echternacht
University of Missouri-Columbia — Columbia, Missouri

Chapter 6

Ken Quamme
University of North Dakota - Williston — Williston, North Dakota

Kent Quamme
Fergus Falls Community College — Fergus Falls, Minnesota

Chapter 7

William C. Ward, III
Kent State University - Trumbull Campus — Warren, Ohio

Chapter 8

Robert J. Matyska, Jr.
University of South Carolina — Columbia, South Carolina

Chapter 9

Bobbye J. Davis
Southeastern Louisiana University — Hammond, Louisiana

Josie V. Walker
Southeastern Louisiana University — Hammond, Louisiana

Chapter 10

Margaret J. Erthal
Southern Illinois University — Edwardsville, Illinois

Chapter 11

part III Internet-Related Visions and Topics

Chapter 12

Chapter 13

Chapter 14

Chapter 15

History and Policies

Chapter 1 — Vignettes in the History of the Internet

by Jay Stephens
Carbon School District — Price, Utah

Matt's face was brilliant in the glory of public recognition of his recent work at school. He was being awarded the "Outstanding Student of the Quarter." For years he had been lost in the mediocrity of his own disinterest, but this year, touched by a master teacher, Matt had found the excitement of learning.

One reason many stay in education is to watch the passion ignite in students as they capture the fire and drive of a successful learning event. As an educator, you have crafted activities that immersed your students in successful learning experiences, and you have probably created a few activities that, politely stated, were less successful.

Wouldn't it be great if we could all share each other's finest activities? Consider the impact of collecting 20,000 of the most successful learning activities from across the nation and making them available to your students. Among them there might be one that would capture the attention of the student you could not reach, or another that might reinforce a concept for a struggling student that had exhausted your repertoire. Now, add to that the power of communicating with the author of that activity, or interacting with other students using same activity. The possibility of such sharing is the dream of the Internet. In the chapters that follow, you will glimpse some of the shared creativity made possible by the Internet.

Mean Time-to-Failure

Failure has often marked the steps of progress in our fast-paced, high tech era. Through our suffering, we learn and move on. If Thomas Edison was not the author of this learning style, he at least understood it: "Results? I have results, I now know 9,000 ways not to make a light bulb."

In 1858, after months of difficult work laying the first transatlantic cable, instantaneous communication across the ocean was established. The transatlantic cable remained in service only a few days before it failed. Technically, it was a failure. However, the lessons learned from the first cable made subsequent efforts completely successful and initiated the era of global telecommunications. In the following years, other transatlantic cables were completed that remained in service for nearly 100 years.

Another failure heralded the beginning of the Internet. In September 1969, Professor Kleinrock at the University of California, Los Angeles (UCLA), initiated the first login over the newly established Network Measurement Center. Under the Defense Advanced Research Project Agency (DARPA) network, UCLA, Stanford Research Institute (SRI), the University of California, Santa Barbara (UCSB), and the University of Utah set up the first four computers of the project. The small group of researchers and graduate students at UCLA hoped to log on to the SRI computer to send data. The *Knight-Ridder Newspaper* recorded Dr. Kleinrock's interview:

> We set up telephone connections between us (at UCLA) and SRI. We
> typed **L** and we asked on the phone, "Do you see the **L**?"
> "Yes, we see the **L**," was the response from SRI.
> We typed the **O** and we asked, "Do you see the **O**?"
> "Yes, we see the **O**."
> We typed the **G** and the system crashed!

While the task of the day was a failure, the Internet had begun! The advance of technology has been breathtaking, but each step is based on the painful lessons learned from the previous step. However, knowing that we are progressing is of little consolation when the most feared words, "The server crashed!" echo through your classroom.

Computer-Mediated Communications

The DARPAnet established electronic messaging as the earliest and most popular service on the Internet. Scientists could relay quick observations and notes without the cumbersome process of transferring files. Stewart Brand, in his *II Cybernetic Frontiers*, published by Random House, 1974, stated:

> There is a curious mix of theoretical fascination and operational
> resistance around the scheme (the Internet). The resistance may have
> something to do with reluctances about equipping a future "Big
> Brother" and his "Central Computer." The fascination resides in the
> thorough rightness of computers as communication instruments,
> which implies some revolutions.

The exchange of technical information spawned the growth of e-mail. These early e-mail programs used "clunky" line editors that were anything but easy. The sophistication of e-mail programs increased as the population of e-mail users expanded. Multiple destination addresses, subject line for filtering desired messages, editing features for preparing mail, and the file attachments added functionality to e-mail and made it appealing to a much larger group, including students. With students, online e-mail began to service two needs:

- Propagating information to a distributed group; and

- Social interaction that was generally much more personal.

It was an exciting mix of personal and mass media communications.

Besides communications, work groups found ways to use e-mail to simplify tasks. Scheduling in any group has always been a problem. E-mail techniques were developed that permitted members of the group to maintain a common calendar. Members could quickly check the calendar for available times to plan meetings or conference calls. Group productivity tools are now available that have expanded this simple calendaring process to include resource and document management. Future Internet productivity tools will include many traditional desktop applications like word processing, spreadsheets, and database management.

E-mail has also nurtured a new class of employee — the telecommuter. Many areas of the United States that are prone to heavy air pollution have looked at telecommuting as a possible solution to reduce the number of vehicles on the road. Under the governor's decree, the state government of Utah is using telecommuting to help reduce by 20 percent the miles driven by state workers both on the job and commuting to and from work.

Information, Power, and Politics

In 1988, under the reforms of Mikhail Gorbachev, the Kurchatov Institute of Atomic Energy established the first Soviet computer network to connect UNIX programmers. In August 1990, they expanded with a link to the European Union network and the rest of the world. By August of 1991, they were providing service to 70 major Soviet cities and 200,000 users. It is ironic to observe that in the United States, many bulletin board services (BBSs) were established as anti-establishment, anti-free market, independent voices, but in Russia the BBSs were established as anti-establishment, pro-free market voices to support commercial activity.

On August 19, 1991, Gennady I. Yanagev, the Russian Vice President to Gorbachev, and the self-appointed, eight member "State of Emergency Committee" dispatched the military to control the mass media and key national centers in a traditional coup d'etat. They forced state-sanctioned programming and news reports. However, they failed to recognize the computer networks and the Internet as a means of mass communication. Hundreds of individuals from around Russia used the Internet to keep the West and each other informed about the details of what was and what was not happening. Not only could individuals reproduce and publish local government decrees, they could also add their own editorials and analysis. The individual perspective added credibility to the ongoing reports. On the final day of the coup, there were over 13,000 individual postings to newsgroups and listservs. The coup leaders were forced to deal with world opinion that was well-informed and unanimously opposed to them. Thanks to the Internet, the coup had failed to control the flow of information.

"The thorough rightness of computers as communications instruments implies some revolutions," prophesied Steward Brand in 1974. There is another revolution that may have more impact on us than the failed Soviet coup. Alvin and Heidi Toffler describe an extensive restructuring of society in their book, *Creating a New Civilization*. The Tofflers explain that hierarchical organizations designed for the manufacturing age will not be able to deal with the demands of individualization and customization required to be successful and competitive in the information age. For example, traditional school structures have grouped teachers with a common content area into departments, the departments into schools, and the schools into districts. Support came through these organizations. With dynamic technology, these organizations have not been able to keep up with the needs for technical support.

The Internet permits an educator to create a support group that focuses on a specific area of concern. This virtual support could include corporate professionals or teachers in other schools, districts, or countries that may have expertise relevant to the teacher's needs. One such innovative project began in mid-1996 with Microsoft Corporation, South-Western Educational Publishing Company, and the Center for Electronic Education and Evaluation (CEEE) linking software developers, textbook authors, publishers, and evaluation/training specialists with classroom teachers to provide a virtual support system. Through Internet Distance Education (IDE), cadres of teachers and content experts exchange problems, solutions, and enjoy social interaction.

Growth

Estimating the size of the Internet is extremely difficult because there is no central registration of Internet users. However, to assure unique names, there is a procedure to register domain names. Based on the registered domain names, at least an estimate of the number of host computers on the Internet can be established.

The early years of the Internet served a small population of researchers. In 1969, there were only four computers, and under Advanced Research Projects Agency (ARPA) and DARPA, the Net grew slowly. In 1984, just prior to the National Science Foundation's (NSF) involvement, there were about 1,000 host computers. With NSF funding, the growth accelerated; in 1987 there were 28,000 hosts and by 1992 there were one million. It took 23 years to connect the first one million. In 1989, NSF announced that it would reduce funding by 20 percent each year for the next five years.

As these funds were reduced, local computer centers were forced to limit services or explore alternative methods of funding. Because terms of the NFS funding prohibited commercial use of the Internet, there were few businesses that were interested in funding a computer network that they could not use. The restrictions on commercial use were eased as the level of funding from NSF decreased. By March of 1994, the NSF completely withdrew its funding, and the great metamorphosis from a research and educational network to a commercial network began. By the end of 1994, there were 3.8 million host computers; in 1995, over nine million, and at the end of 1996 there were over 12 million.

The number of users is nearly impossible to establish. Various statistical methods have been used to estimate the number of users, but the different methods generate very different numbers. The estimated number of users in 1996 range from nine to 35 million. The surveys also bring out interesting demographic information. Thirty percent of the users are educators and 28 percent have computer-related jobs.

The unparalleled growth of the Internet has captured everyone's attention. In 1993, the Web browser population increased 341,634 percent. In anyone's book, that kind of growth means power and money. Telecommunications companies are spending billions of dollars to improve network access and connections. Software companies are investing heavily in developing new software products that take advantage of the resources available on the Internet and related Intranets. Many large entertainment companies are looking for partners or smaller companies they can purchase to gain the necessary expertise to successfully deliver a new generation of multimedia, interactive entertainment. The term "edutainment" has been coined to mark the birth of a new industry focused on delivering educational content in a style that modern entertainment consumers, often referred to as the "Nintendo Generation," have grown to expect and demand.

Your Classroom

The most critical event in the history of the Internet may still need to be written — the connection of your classroom. Educators will need to learn several new skills:

- How to create and use interactive multimedia activities;
- How to work with groups of other educators as a team;
- How to build their own technical or curriculum support networks; and
- How to facilitate their students' learning even if the students exceed the skill and knowledge of the educators.

INTERACTIVE ACTIVITIES. Traditional classroom activities are often based on printed media and require a student to respond to simulated questions, case studies, or problems from the business world. We need to envision a whole new approach to delivering training, using multiple mediums of presentation, and requiring students to respond using multimedia.

WORK IN TEAMS. The creation of a new generation of multimedia curricula is a massive undertaking that is overpowering if it has to be done by individual teachers. The Microsoft Corporation, South-Western Educational

Publishing Company, and CEEE project is one example of the virtual teams we need to build. The Academy of Multimedia in Utah is another project that has brought together teams of teachers, students, and industry specialists to build Internet-ready curriculum activities that will have a major impact on the educational process. The technology is here to end the isolation of the classroom and to build support teams to better meet the needs of our students.

FACILITATE. With the new generation of training comes the frightening realization that many of the concepts taught in the activities may be beyond the technical skill level of the instructor. In the past generation, it was unthinkable to have an instructor that did not have full mastery of every aspect of the content. In today's technically sophisticated environment, it is equally unthinkable that anyone can have full mastery of all aspects of the content. Instructors need to be willing to accept that they cannot know everything, but that experts are available to them on their support network.

The instructor becomes a facilitator that has full mastery of educating and creating an environment conducive to student success. There are additional benefits to the facilitator model of instruction. For example, students confined to home because of illness, behavior, or relocation can continue their training and studies over the Internet. Facilitated instruction has the possibility of enhancing student learning without regard to time or distance. Any student, any time of day or night, from anywhere in the world can access training material and work with his or her teacher.

Facilitated instruction consists of three steps that every educator should take. First, a teacher must get connected to the Internet and then resolve to help students get access. Second, a teacher needs to review his or her repertoire of activities and select the finest activities with the intention of making them Internet ready. And finally, a teacher must work with other educators, business/industry specialists, and students to create a shared set of activities that have relevance in today's business world.

A Detailed Time Line

There are many excellent articles about the history of the Internet on the Internet (see Table 1). You may use your favorite Internet search engine to look for "Internet History" and read extensive details on many of the entries that follow.

1865 — THE CABLE

- The first transatlantic cable was completed for communications. It was in service for only a few days before it failed, but in 1866 subsequent cables were laid that remained in service for almost 100 years.

1945 — MEMEX

- Vannevar Bush (science advisor to President Roosevelt) proposed a conceptual machine that could store vast amounts of information where users would have the ability to create information trails — links of related text and illustrations. Bush called for a new relationship

Table 1: Resources for the History of the Internet

- The Internic is the source of all formal domain name registrations and related information.
  - ftp://rs.internic.net
- This is a comprehensive history. Look for the link "History of the Internet: The Roads and Crossroads of Internet's History."
  - http://www.internetvalley.com
- This is an extensive treatment of the Internet, including a definition of the term Internet, with a bibliography.
  - http://info.isoc.org
- The Federation of American Scientists has a collection of Internet statistics. Try their search tool to locate them.
  - http://www.fas.org

between thinking man and the sum of knowledge. This became the conceptual foundation of the World Wide Web and Hypertext links.

1957 — ARPA
- President Eisenhower organized the Advanced Research Projects Agency. In the early 1960s, ARPA funded between five and eight million dollars for computer research.

1965 — HYPERTEXT
- Ted Nelson coined the term "Hypertext."

1969 — ARPANET
- ARPAnet started by connecting various computers around the country. Computers were expensive, and sharing was the only way to give computing access to many researchers. Around Labor Day, researchers demonstrated a four node network connecting SRI, UCSB, UCLA, and the University of Utah in Salt Lake City. ARPAnet survived because of the perceived need to be able to survive a catastrophe, such as a foreign military invasion. Every computer can know of every other computer and send packets of information to their destination via the quickest route, taking into account that a section of the network might be "bombed out" or simply damaged by a construction crew.

1979 — USENET
- Graduate students at Duke University linked several UNIX machines together to share information. This was a grassroots development created by users, not organizations. The attitude of sharing on the Internet is due largely to the influence of this group. There was no formal organization.

1980 — ARPANET
- In the 1980s ARPAnet split into two networks:

1. APRAnet, for research and commercial military contractors; and
2. The military's Milnet, which was dedicated to military traffic.

- World Wide Web. The Center for High Energy Particle Physics (CERN, Switzerland) became the largest Internet site in Europe and was Tim Berners-Lee's medium used to create the World Wide Web. Berners-Lee wrote a notebook program, "Inquire-Within-Upon-Everything," which permitted links between arbitrary nodes. In 1989, this was developed into a proposal for information management with Hypertext links.

1981 — BITNET

- The City University of New York and Yale University were networked using IBM mainframes. In 1984, 100 organizations and 225 computers were on Bitnet. By 1994, there were 1,400 organizations in 49 countries. Most users were universities or other research organizations. They were governed by an executive committee, and they used a proprietary NJE protocol.

- That same year, Ted Nelson conceptualized his Xanadu Hypertext database. In 1988, Autodesk purchased the project, invested five million dollars, and then dropped it in 1992. The Japanese picked it up and created the Sapporo HyperLab in 1994.

1986 — NSFNET

- The NSF connected five supercomputers. E-mail soon dominated the supercomputer usage. NSF contracted with MCI, IBM, and Merit to manage and upgrade the Net. Universities were encouraged to provide wide access. NSFNet eventually supplanted the ARPA. ARPA retired in March 1990, after 21 years.

1987 — BITNET

- BitNet became a nonprofit organization.

1989 — CREN

- BitNet merged with CSNet, the Computer Science Network, and changed its name to CREN, the Corporation for Research and Educational Networking.

1990 — WORLD WIDE WEB (WWW)

- In November, the initial program was developed by the CERN group on a NeXT computer. Tim Berners-Lee became the hero of the Web revolution, and Steve Jobs the hero of the PC revolution. In the Web's first generation, Berners-Lee launched the Uniform Resource Locator (URL), Hypertext Transfer Protocol (HTTP), and Hypertext Markup Language (HTML) standards.

1991 — NREN

- Al Gore successfully campaigned for the National Research and Education Network or supercomputing legislation.

- Java. Sun Microsystems began working on a programming language for consumer electronics devices — televisions, VCRs, toasters, and so forth. The project did not receive much commercial attention.

1993 — MOSAIC

- In February, NCSA at the University Illinois-Urbana Champaign, released the first alpha version of Marc Andreessen's "Mosaic for X." By October, there were 200 HTTP servers.

9

1994 — COMMERCIAL INTERNET

- In March, the NSF funding ended, and the Internet had to cover all its own expenses.

- Netscape. Marc Andreessen and colleagues left NCSA and formed Mosaic Communications Corporation, now Netscape.

- VRML. In May, the First International WWW Conference was convened at CERN. Virtual Reality Markup Language (VRML) was conceived.

- Hot Java. Sun Microsystems revived the old Java consumer products development language, and released it as Hot Java for downloading and running applets on the Internet.

- WWW. In December, CERN was forced to discontinue WWW development due to budget constraints. The WebCore project was transferred to the "Institut National pour la Rechereche en Informatique et Automatique" (INRIA) in France.

1995 — THE WEB SOCIETY

- In June, the Web Society was founded in Graz by the Technical University of Graz, CERN, the University of Minnesota, and INRA. The Web is one of the fastest growing segments of the Internet because it promised to revolutionize the ways in which people published and retrieved information. Never before have people been able to combine into one document all different types of electronic data — still images, film, video clips, sound clips, and text — and have it so easily accessible to many users in such a consistent, comprehensible way.

1996 — COMMERCIAL DEVELOPMENTS

- Every major software and hardware vendor recognized the significance of the Internet and focused future developments on the new environment.

- Java again. Sun announced a Java standard and a standard setting committee.

- Web TVs and NETPCs. Several major software and hardware companies announced simple computers that would connect directly to the Internet. They ranged in price and function from a very simple $300 set, that connected a television to the Net, to a $2,000 system, that also had full stand-alone functionality, but was configured for Internet services.

Chapter 2 — Acceptable Use Policy

by Billie J. Herrin
University of Montana — Missoula, Montana
and
Jon Robinson
University of Montana — Missoula, Montana

Information technology has had a tremendous effect on education and the ways in which information is accessed in the classroom. The Information Age is evolving so rapidly that educators must continue to develop a supportive environment in which technology is made readily available to students.

The Internet is a form of transitional technology that will enable students to gain access to information for all areas of study. In order to take advantage of the information that is available through the Internet, teachers will need to continually update their knowledge base of technology and the Internet. They will then be able to teach students how to use the Internet, and they will also be able to control information accessed and retrieved by students.

Because of the need for control, most schools are developing both Board and Acceptable Use Policies (AUPs). AUPs help to define acceptable behaviors by student and staff users of information systems. Board Policies take this much further. They describe acceptable student behaviors and also tie those standards to the district's policies on students' rights and responsibilities (McKenzie, 1995).

This chapter will explore the historical perspective of educational networks, describe the need for AUPs and Board Policies, suggest ways to develop an AUP and Board Policy, illustrate a good AUP design, and look at the future implications of AUPs on business education.

Historical Review of Acceptable Use Policies

The first computers used in classrooms were mostly stand-alone systems. The teacher decided what software would be installed and then closely supervised student use. As personal computers became more common and more powerful, business teachers started to network their computer classrooms to better represent the work environment. Networking made maintenance easier and allowed resources such as printers to be shared. Even when the classrooms were open for general lab purposes, the teachers had fairly strict control over the software installed on each computer and the uses that were allowed.

12

As electronic means of communication and especially electronic mail and conferencing became more popular, states, districts, schools, and other educational entities began creating computer bulletin board systems (BBSs) to help facilitate communication. The benefits for teachers, particularly those isolated from peers, were incalculable. Allowing students access to BBSs introduced new forms of group interaction and learning. Most of these BBSs were especially designed for a K-12 audience and the material found on them was maintained by local system operators (sysop(s)).

The sysops could generally guarantee that information accessed was acceptable for most students. This control changed, however, when distributed conferencing networks became more prominent. The nature of distributed conferencing, such as USENet and FIDONet, began to make monitoring BBSs more difficult. Few problems were encountered, however, because of the small number of people with access to BBSs at that time. Conference moderators and teachers were able to keep control of most online activities.

The Internet has dramatically changed this situation. While the value of Internet access for K-12 schools is undeniable, the open and ubiquitous nature of the Internet and World Wide Web (WWW) has made it much more difficult for districts or schools to control the resources accessed by computers. Most educators agree that a carefully designed curriculum, which engages students in specific task-oriented educational pursuits on the Internet, is the best way to focus student interests away from non-educational material. In an elementary education setting this may be easy to accomplish, but in secondary educational institutions it is difficult to monitor. Willard (1996) stated that allowing students Internet access, but not allowing personal exploration time would be similar to establishing a school library and then telling students they can only use the library for class projects.

Safdar and Cherry (1996) discussed various methods of controlling content, focusing on software-based options such as author-based and third-party rating systems. Software that works in conjunction with rating systems, such as Cyberpatrol and Surfwatch, can help schools in limiting access to objectionable material. Because sites change so rapidly and hundreds of new ones open their doors each day, schools cannot solely rely on content filters to successfully block inappropriate material. Districts, administrators, teachers, and parents must come to some agreement about what is and what is not appropriate use of a school's computing system and resources. Such an agreement must be defined in writing.

Acceptable Use Policies

Faced with the need to define acceptable use and present it in a written form, districts and schools have developed AUPs. A properly designed and implemented AUP must take into account the privileges, rights, and responsibilities of network usage. For a better understanding of the scope and purpose of an AUP, its three parts will be discussed. The first section covers the rules for acceptable use and the punishment that must be determined by the school's or district's administrators and the school board. The second section is a conduct guide, which covers rules that are less strict. This section is often referred to as the "netiquette" guide. The third section usually contains a form or letter, similar to a field trip permission slip, which is signed by students and parents, unless the student is 18 years of age, acknowledging that they are aware of the conduct guidelines and the capability of their child accessing inappropriate material via the school network.

SECTION ONE. The AUPs should become part of the Board Policies, which are then codified and included in the school handbook. These rules can often be drawn from similar preexisting rules. The punishment for sending a teacher a threatening e-mail message, for example, should be similar to that for threatening the teacher in person or in a written note. The student who creates or purposely disseminates a computer virus to the school's network or even out to the Internet should suffer the same consequences as one who vandalizes school property. Determining who can set up and maintain Web pages on the network would be another issue that might be addressed in a Board Policy.

Easy-to-use Web page authoring and site hosting software, such as Microsoft's Front Page make it possible for teachers or computer literate students to set up a Web server. Because the machine name would identify it with the school or district, the administration may want to place certain limits on the content or require a notice on the page(s) which state that the content does not necessarily represent the opinions or views of the school district. This is increasingly important when students in extracurricular clubs and activities set up, create, and maintain pages for their clubs on a central Web server.

SECTION TWO. A "netiquette" guide should provide basic rules and guidelines for conduct on the local network and also for Internet use at large. Typical guidelines include:

- Keep messages short; and
- Be careful when using sarcasm or humor online as they can be easily misinterpreted.

Other issues that the "netiquette" guide should address are ones such as student safety. It is important that students do not give out personal information such as their home address or telephone number to people they meet on the Internet, or publish them on Web pages. They should also be warned not to agree to a meeting with anyone they meet via the network without parental supervision. Including a "netiquette" point giving them someone to turn to if they feel uncomfortable, such as, "if you feel uncomfortable with the tone or nature of an online conversation please report it to your teacher" may help to prevent a problem from occurring.

SECTION THREE. The final section is a letter to the parents advising them of their child's access and their rights and responsibilities. Interpretation of the letter by parents and students is very important, therefore, the message should be concise and clear. The message generally begins with an explanation of the Internet and reasons for providing student access. Examples such as providing access to NASA space images for a science class, using CNN's news stories in a current event lesson, or finding information about the culture of Thailand to prepare a report on international business for a business communication class may give parents and students a clearer understanding of information available through the Internet.

While the AUP should contain some information and possibly examples of various Board Policies, it should always point back to relevant sections of the school handbook for further information. Students should always realize that Internet access is a privilege not a right, and access is provided specifically for educational use. Length and detail of the AUP may vary. Elementary students will most likely not have a private e-mail account, and they will rarely be allowed unsupervised exploration time. In cases such as these, a short note instead of a letter to the parents may suffice.

Parents should always have the choice of prohibiting Internet access for their child. Most often this is accomplished by having the parents sign the acceptable use letter if they do want to allow access, or by not signing and signifying their refusal in that way. One way in which AUPs can be presented to parents is to invite them to a "technology night" at the school. Parents and students could learn together about the Internet and how it can be used in the classroom. It also allows for the AUP to be presented and letters to be signed and collected in a convenient manner.

Developing an AUP

Reasons for developing good AUPs are numerous. While content monitoring software can help prevent access to non-educational materials, multitudinous objections to their use are found. The software can be expensive to implement and monitor on a large school or district network. Doing so might draw away financial resources that could instead be spent on training or better equipment. The main objection, however, is that monitoring software creates a false sense of security. Content monitors cannot block everything deemed objectionable because of the fast-changing nature of the Internet. Determining what is and what is not objectionable can be difficult.

Some schools or districts may want to block material dealing with chemical reactions because of the well-known documents on explosives manufacturing available on the Internet. Another school with an advanced chemistry class, however, may decide that blocking out such material would hinder research by students. School districts in different areas of the country will deem different subject matters objectionable. Including computer ethics and responsibility in the curriculum, therefore, will help students more clearly understand what is acceptable in their school.

Certain subjects may be appropriate for high school or middle school students yet inappropriate for elementary students. Monitoring the Internet traffic of all children is virtually impossible for schools. Responsibility for monitoring should not be placed solely on the educational system. Parents must also be encouraged to participate. Willard (1996) stated that providing students with access to the Internet presents an excellent opportunity to encourage parents to have a discussion with their child about family values and what their expectations are for their child's activities while on the Internet. The strongest argument for content monitoring is that it shows a good faith effort by the school district to limit access to clearly objectionable material (Willard, 1996).

The next issue is censorship and where and at what level it should be applied. While it is reasonable for schools to block certain kinds of information (text, graphics, or other electronic communications), the importance of free speech should be respected. Willard (1996) pointed out that students do not shed their constitutional rights to freedom of speech or expression at the schoolhouse gate, as realized in the Tinker v. Des Moines Independent Community School District, 393 U. S. 503, 506, (1969) case. Students also do not shed their constitutional rights on the school district's on-ramp to the Information Superhighway. A good guide to follow is the *Intellectual Freedom Manual* published by the American Library Association, Office for Intellectual Freedom (1992).

Schools or districts will want to implement rules on various uses of the Internet that content filters do not monitor. Downloading various software, including games, may be one example. While there are many useful software packages available from the Internet, there is considerable danger from downloading virus-infected software. Because of this danger, some districts may want to prohibit the downloading of software by anyone other than their computer department personnel. Some schools might allow anyone to download software but prohibit anyone to download or install games or software judged non-educational. The AUP letter should allude to some of the issues and regulations, but these should be addressed in a broader context in the Board Policy.

Privacy is another issue AUPs should address. Most networks include documentation language that gives network administrators the authorization to read private files on their network in order to maintain the system. Likewise, users should be made aware that personal files, including e-mail, can be searched if there is reason to believe that a law or rule may have been broken. Schools may want to include additional regulations or policies which state that parents are allowed access to their child's private e-mail upon request of the network administrator. Instituting such policies will help clarify what is proper and acceptable use.

AUPs should also address network security issues. Security must be considered both from the vantage of protecting the school's network and protecting the Internet. Both "netiquette" and Board Policy should address the issue that a user's password should be held with the greatest secrecy and should never be given out or written down in an obvious place. Other rules that should be clearly outlined in AUPs and Board Policies include:

- "Hacking" into another person's account or other computers connected through the Internet.
- Knowingly creating or downloading viruses.
- Deliberately hindering network performance.

Samples of Good Acceptable Use and Board Policies

The wheel does not need to be reinvented when it comes to AUPs. Schools can access AUPs and many other valuable resources online. Listed below is a sampling of sites to explore:

- url http://www.rice.edu/armadillo/Rice/Resources/acceptable.html
- gopher://riceinfor.rice.edu:1170/More/Acceptable
- http://www.bham.wednet.edu
- http://fileroom.aaup.uic.edu/FileRoom/documents/homepage.html
- http://www.eff.org/CAF/cafuiuc.html
- http://webcrawler.com—search for Schools, AUPs such as ftp://ftp.classroom.net/wentworth/Classroom-Connect/aup
- http://www.erehwon.com/k12aup
- http://www.io.com/%7Ekinnaman/aupessay.html
- http://cosn.org/people/pfaffman/rfc1578.html—this site will lead to many educational addresses
- http://larrysworld.com/child_safety.html

AUPS. As previously described, an AUP is a local policy document that outlines the terms and conditions of a school or district's Internet usage plan. The policy should explain what the Internet is, how teachers and students will be accessing it, how the Internet will be used in the classroom, and what rights and responsibilities users agree to when signing an AUP. The AUP needs to:

- Outline in concise, clear language that students at all levels understand guidelines for what is appropriate access when online;
- Spell out consequences for violations to the policy;
- State rules of online behavior and access privileges;
- Reflect the values of the population which it serves; and
- Require a signature of parents/guardians, teacher, and student — see Table 1 — (*Classroom Connect Newsletter*, December 1994, January 1995). Many document samples are now available online.

Table 1: AUP for XYZ High School

XYZ High School's access to the Internet provides benefits to students, teachers, administrators, and staff in our school. Our goal in providing this service is to promote educational excellence by facilitating resource sharing, exploration, innovation, and communication through our direct Internet connection. The Internet is an electronic hookup to millions of computers and individuals in the world. With this access comes the availability of material that may not be considered to be of educational value. Special precautions have been taken and XXX software restricts access to controversial materials. The use of computers and Internet access is a privilege and not a right. We require that all students, parents/guardians, and teachers sign a binding agreement which acknowledges that they have read the terms and conditions of acceptable use and understand their inherent responsibilities.

Rules of Conduct

1. Use of school computers is limited to educational purposes.
2. Personal privacy must be protected. Use of personal information must not be revealed (i.e., addresses and phone numbers).
3. Discriminatory or obscene language is prohibited.
4. Harassing, insulting, or attacking others is prohibited.
5. Sending or displaying offensive messages or pictures is prohibited.
6. Copyrighted material must not be downloaded without the author's permission. Only authorized system operators will be allowed to download or install programs to the system.
7. E-mail is not guaranteed to be private. System administrators may need to access files for the maintenance of the computer facilities.
8. Vandalism of any kind will result in termination of computer privileges. Vandalism is defined as any attempt to harm or damage computers, computer systems, or computer networks or to infiltrate another computer system. This includes creating or uploading computer viruses.
9. Any user who does not choose to comply with the Rules of Conduct will lose computer privileges for a period of time to be determined by Board Policy. Repeated infractions may result in permanent termination of computer and/or Internet privileges. Standard disciplinary procedures of XYZ High School will apply.

I have read the rules for acceptable online behavior and agree to comply with these rules. Should I violate these rules, my computer privileges at XYZ High School may be revoked.

_____

Student Signature   Date

As the parent or legal guardian of this student, I have read this policy and agree to the terms.

_____

Parent/Guardian   Date

I have read the AUP and agree to promote this agreement with the student.

_____

Teacher's Signature   Date

Sources:
http://www.classroom.net/wentworth/classroom-Connect.
gopher://riceinfo.rice.edu:1170/MoreAcceptable.
Missoula County Public School's Acceptable Use Policy, Missoula, Montana.

17

Table 1 is an example of a clear and concise AUP and is developed from several AUP resources available today. Each school or district should determine the best document to fit the needs, location, philosophy, and population of its school and then develop its own or use one of the many available. As previously stated, the wheel does not need to be reinvented.

18

BOARD POLICIES. Board Policies are more comprehensive than AUPs. They echo the content of AUPs and also tie those standards to the district's policies on student rights and responsibilities and acceptable student behaviors. They may, for example, tie the district policy and procedures on student locker searches and student's rights to privacy or freedom of speech to the policies of the AUP. A sound Board Policy may take a position on access to potentially controversial information and relate new Internet sources to pre-existing policies on curriculum and the selection of curriculum materials. Outlining clear expectations for staff supervision of student use is very important. Finally, Board Policies should also outline a comprehensive set of policies which describe staff responsibilities and rights as employees using these utilities (*From Now On*, 1995).

Risks are involved if School Boards or Boards of Public Education remain silent and uninvolved in AUP and Board Policy development. Many people are unprepared for the serious values conflicts which may arise if boards remain silent. Restrictive legislation can encourage all kinds of censorship and heavy-handed regulation by groups and individuals. The more ambiguous the rules, the greater the risk that individuals will be caught in storms of protest or moral dilemmas (*From Now On*, 1995).

Since risks are associated with attempts to launch surveillance efforts, a good Board Policy should address the following:

- Contact with objectionable material.
- Contact with questionable material.
- Contact with questionable persons.
- Objectionable behavior.
- Objectional material.
- Destructive behavior.
- Violation of privacy rights.
- Violation of access rights (*From Now On*, 1995).

Other topics to be addressed in a Board Policy include the schools' philosophical stance, school/home responsibilities, staff responsibilities, and student responsibilities. The policy should address such philosophical stances as:

- How the delivery of information is changing in our society.
- What relationship the new information technologies and resources have to the district's selection and screening of instructional materials.

- What the proper relationship is between information and student learning (*From Now On*, 1995).

School/home responsibilities require the Board Policy to cover such issues as:

- How much supervision students require at various age levels.
- Who provides supervision and how this should be done.
- Who decides which information sources are acceptable, parents or the school.

Staff responsibility issues might cover such topics as:

- What roles of teachers, administrators, or library media specialists are appropriate.
- How the prescreening of sites and materials are handled.
- How guidance is different from censorship.
- Who should teach new research skills and blend the new kinds of research throughout the curriculum.

Student responsibility issues addressed might include:

- What constitutes responsible behavior and communication.
- What the connection is to existing codes and procedures.
- How much privacy students can expect.
- What restrictions, if any, should be placed on freedom of speech (*From Now On*, 1995).

Enacting Board Policies can curtail Internet "fire storms" similar to those created for library and textbook censorship situations. Issues of these types can be resolved at a philosophical level by the Board as representative of community values. Board Policies can help tie all school standards together (*From Now On*, 1995).

AUPs and Future Implications for Business Education

Business Educators must continue to be at the forefront of researching new addresses and sites on the Internet. Because of the many envisioned changes in Internet access every year, they must also be professionally responsible in helping other educators, administrators, and staff continually update the AUPs in their schools.

Leiken (1996) stated that teachers will need to be guides on the new online frontier to make the Internet a useful learning tool. They will extract the quality from the Web's expanding quantity and apply it for new and enriching learning opportunities. With the teacher's guidance, the Internet's vast resources can be transformed into a virtual, interactive, and collaborative global classroom (Leiken 1996).

EFFECTS ON TEACHING AND RESEARCH. President Bill Clinton declared during his January 23, 1996, State of the Union Address, that by the year 2000 every classroom in America must be connected to the Information Superhighway, with computers, software, and well-trained teachers. He further stated that the government is working with the telecommunications industry, educators, and parents to ensure that every classroom and every library in the entire United States will be connected by the year 2000 (Leiken, 1996).

20

Leiken (1996) asserted that the Internet is the greatest phenomenon in education technology since the overhead projector. Educators must ask themselves:

- What can the Internet and WWW do for education?
- How will access affect teaching, curricula, and the role of the teacher in the classroom?

Teachers have found that the WWW creates new levels of individualization and encourages collaborations that take students far beyond the classroom.

What teachers and students need is a guide that points to online educational resources such as documents, photographs, maps, video clips, sound bites, references, and teaching materials for every level and content area. There is a compendium of online educational resources available for all educators which includes lesson plan collections; curriculum resources from schools, colleges, government agencies, and commercial organizations; cooperative online projects; and Web-based libraries, museums, and communications media (Dyrli, 1996).

Many textbook publishers are developing manuals, workbooks, yellow pages, and other sources for use in finding interesting Internet sites related to business education. Students in many business classes can quickly search and access information on any topic related to business courses. This allows immediate retrieval from historical to up-to-the-minute information. Business educators need to assure students that access to such sources will remain available.

FUTURE RESTRICTIONS AND IMPLICATIONS. Future implications include looking at ways in which Internet access will change our teaching environment. As the 21st century nears, Internet offerings and changes will be occurring daily. Some of these changes are presupposed in a statement by Peter Magrath (1997):

> Current conceit says that Internet time must be reckoned in dog years. The pace of change is so fast that one year on the Internet is like seven years in any other medium. By this scheme, it has been nearly a century since the Internet was born. It has been 14 years since the emergence of the WWW as an electronic-publishing vehicle. And by the year 2000, the Internet will have undergone another two decades' worth of growth and development. (p. 82)

The original goal of the Internet in the 1960s was a sharing of resources. The Internet, however, soon evolved into a system for the exchange of messages and documents, thus, giving rise to e-mail. After the advent of eail exchange, the Internet became a reference medium where research apers could be easily read by anyone on the network.

More and more changes are occurring daily. At the end of 1996, ccording to Jupiter Communications, a New York-based research and consulting firm, more than 15 million North American households had some form of nline access. By the year 2000, projections estimate that more than 38 iillion homes in the United States will have online access — more than one-iird of all households (Magrath, 1997).

Magrath (1997) stated that this move to Infotopia has become more ostly than expected. Devout early users of the Internet believed in the roposition that all information should be free, and this attitude still prevails. *he Wall Street Journal*, for example, began charging a subscription fee for the nline edition and soon saw a dramatic decline in online readership.

Writing additions to AUPs to cover such access fees for students or staff ould be inexplicably difficult to manage. If educational institutions were iarged fees to access educational sites, they would soon have to drop online ervices.

If students have access to all the new Internet sites and offerings from ieir homes, how will this affect their access to sites at school? Parents will ertainly need to be aware of the information being accessed from home omputers. Schools and system operators will need to evaluate continually ie software they are using to determine if it adequately filters access to ertain sites. The system operators will also need to explore continually the ew areas and capabilities of the Internet to determine if changes need to e noted in the AUP. Schools will certainly not want to deny access to new ducational materials, yet they will want to control access to offensive sites.

In years to come, cyberspace will continue its transformations. A rash of ew personal computer devices, such as Internet televisions and Internet tele-hones, will soon be commonplace. Internet television in particular is a promis-ig device, and will benefit from the growing market in Web-based video games. redictions show that by the year 2000, as new video-compression techniques icrease, the realism of online game-playing will be a hot area (Magrath, 1997). udents love to play video games. If these are downloaded to their school site, ie teachers and staff will need to determine what access students will have to iese games. This will create more implications for AUP changes.

Commerce will also continue to thrive, especially if electronic cash and nart cards allow for micropayments of as little as 25 cents for online con-imer purchases. Schools' AUPs will have to deal with issues related to the udent use of cash or smart cards at school (Magrath, 1997).

All the new sites and technologies will have many implications on iaintaining viable AUPs in schools across our nation. Business educators will eed to be continually involved in policy updating to help their schools etermine what is allowed, and also to determine what sites are good re-urces for educational projects.

References

Acceptable Use Policies: Defining What's Allowed Online, and What's Not. (1994, December/1995, January). *Classroom Connect Newsletter.* [Online]. Available: http://www.wentworth.com/classroom/aup.htm.

American Library Association, Office for Intellectual Freedom (1992). *Intellectual Freedom Manual.* Chicago, IL: Author.

Dyrli, O. E. (1996, October). The Educator's Ultimate World Wide Web Hotlist. *Technology & Learning,* 17, 44-48.

Leiken, E. (1996). The Net: Where It's @. *Techniques — Making Education and Career Connections,* 71, 34-40.

Magrath, P. (1997, January 27). America 2000, the Internet, the Web: Infotopia or Marketplace *Newsweek* 129, 4, 82-84.

McKenzie, J. (1995, May). Creating Board Policies for Student Use of the Internet. *From Now On — May, 1995: A Monthly Electronic Commentary on Educational Technology Issues,* 5, 7, [Online]. Available: http://fromnowon.org.

Sadfar, S. J., and Cherry, S. (1996). *Internet Parental Control Frequently Asked Questions (FAQ)* [Online]. Available: http://www.vtw.org/parents/.

22

Chapter 3 — Policing the Internet: Developing an Acceptable Use Policy

by Wayne A. Moore
Indiana University of Pennsylvania — Indiana, Pennsylvania
and
Raymond Rakvic, Jr.
Norwin High School — North Huntingdon, Pennsylvania

Communication technologies have shifted the way information is accessed, communicated, and transferred by members of society. This has allowed changes, not just in industry, but also in education, influencing instruction and student learning. On February 4, 1997, President Clinton conveyed in his State of the Union Address a boost for education which looked to the 21st Century. He stated:

> *Now, looking ahead, the greatest step of all — the high threshold of the future we now must cross — and my number one priority for the next four years is to ensure that all Americans have the best education in the world.*

He set three goals, one of which was that by age 12 all students should be able to log on to the Internet. This goal would allow students in rural, suburb, and inner city schools to have the same access to the same universe of knowledge.

Access to telecommunications enables students to explore thousands of libraries, databases, and bulletin boards while exchanging messages with individuals from around the world. With any technology there are advantages and disadvantages. Many pioneer teachers who have incorporated telecommunications into the curriculum believe the benefits exceed the disadvantages. A dilemma facing the integration of telecommunications into the curriculum is the ability to screen material students may be searching on the World Wide Web (WWW). In the past, instructional and library media materials were often scrutinized and screened by committees consisting of educators and community members. This process is not so easily handled on the Internet.

Many school districts struggle with questions about providing their staff and students with access to the Internet. The "easy" questions deal with technical issues:

- How does one connect?
- Who will offer the service?
- How much does it cost?

Questions that may be more difficult to answer include:

- How is the Internet used pedagogically?
- Is it worth the cost?
- What are the ramifications if a student accesses information that is racist, sexist, sexually explicit, or otherwise objectionable?

Teachers and parents are becoming increasingly concerned about the appropriateness of some of the materials available to students online and throughout the Internet. Attempts are being made to limit access or "filter" specific resources. Many Internet access providers set their systems to offer users a menu of choices. By controlling what choices appear on the menu, users can be limited to specific services.

The open and interconnected nature of the Internet, however, makes controlling inappropriate use a difficult task. To ensure that there are no questionable materials on a network system, a school would have to utilize either no links to other systems (eliminating the need for Internet access) or make sure that everyone in the world agrees to keep questionable materials out of their systems — a ludicrous request.

Individual users must develop respect for the ideas of others, yet at the same time, protect themselves from others who have not developed a similar respect. Several policies warn the users not to post personal information such as name, address, or phone number. In order to protect schools and reassure parents of the educational value, administrators and technology coordinators must create and implement an Acceptable Use Policy (AUP). An AUP is a written agreement that can be signed by students, parents, and teachers, outlining the terms and conditions of Internet use. It specifically sets out acceptable uses, rules of online behavior, and access privileges. Also covered are penalties for violations of the policy, including security violations and vandalism of the system. Anyone using a school's Internet connection should be required to sign an AUP and know that it will be kept on file as a legally binding document.

It is imperative that school systems educate their faculty and staff on the importance of developing and adhering to an AUP, of understanding the components of the policy, and of identifying when the AUP may need to be revised to meet changes in technological advances and curriculum needs.

Importance of an AUP

Policies should be developed with the involvement of teachers, students, administrators, school and/or district technology coordinator(s), and parents and/or guardians. It may be helpful to invite the participation of one or more ecognized leaders in the community who do not have direct affiliation with he school system, such as advisory committee members.

Before actual policy formulation begins, the policy making group must be educated on the educational goals of the Internet and the importance of developing proper guidelines on the use of the Internet. Guidelines should include:

25

- Policy that is straightforward and easy to understand.

- Education of the staff, students, and parents and/or guardians on the use of the Internet.

- Compilation of sample AUP documents to be used as guides.

- Secure written acknowledgments and consent forms as applicable.

Open communication with students and parents about how the Internet s being used in the classroom is the best way to avoid misunderstandings and undue concern. Schools can accomplish this by holding special technology meetings to introduce students and parents to the Internet. A technology meeting provides a forum for teachers, parents, and students to go over how he Internet will be used in the classroom and to explain the AUP and its ramifications. This special forum can be a step toward informing all parties nvolved on what the Internet is and what information is acceptable to search, when a student can use the Internet, and why students use the Internet. It can also educate parents and students on the enforcement of an AUP and the ramifications if the policy is not followed.

Experience shows that holding technology meetings for parents and students will not reach the total population that will be using the Internet in the school. In addition to several meetings, letters need to be sent home several times informing parents and/or guardians of the possible Internet uses as well as the governing policy. The importance of establishing standards on the use of the Internet is only relevant if the school district can match its mission to the usefulness of providing the service to teachers and students. In understanding the importance of the Internet, there are six areas that should be considered: access, vagueness, enforcement, safety, liability, and privacy.

ACCESS. Access to the Internet will soon be a standard feature of every school computer, whether located in the library, computer lab, or classroom. The Web will be considered an essential tool for student research projects. Sending a letter to parents describing the manner in which students will be able to obtain Internet access, the district's policies regarding student access, and an option for parents to request that children not be allowed access is another approach separate from a technology meeting. Students should not be given access to the Internet without proper permission of the parents and/ or guardians in writing. If students are not given parental permission, alternative work needs to be developed to provide students with the same curricular goals as students on the Internet.

VAGUENESS. A school district must also be concerned with whether the AUP provides clear information to students about what actions will be considered inappropriate and could be sanctioned. Example statements could include, "Students shall not access any objectionable or inappropriate material," or "Students shall not post defamatory, inaccurate, abusive, obscene, profane, sexually-oriented, threatening, offensive, or illegal material." Districts might want to question whether terms such as "objectionable," "inappropriate," "inaccurate," "sexually-oriented," and "offensive" provide a sufficient level of clarity for their students to be able to guide their actions. Prior to students gaining access to the Internet, teachers could use case studies relating to ethical situations to define and clarify terminology that is used in the AUP. Through cooperative learning, students could work in groups exploring the nature of the Internet and its educational value.

ENFORCEMENT. Networking access supports student achievement by fostering appropriate exploration and learning. Students must understand that Internet use is a privilege and not a right. If the privilege is abused, students and parents are clearly educated on the penalties and repercussions of violating the AUP. There are several stakeholders who are all responsible for the enforcement of an AUP including: administrators, teachers, parents, and students.

AUPs may provide a series of penalties for not adhering to the guidelines. Some schools issue a warning letter to students and parents after the first violation — subsequent violations may be cause for access restrictions or suspensions.

Many AUPs include language similar to the following:

The use of the Internet is a privilege, not a right, and inappropriate use will result in a cancellation of those privileges. The system administrator will deem what is inappropriate use and that decision is final. The system administrator may close an account at any time as required. The administration, faculty, and staff may request the administrator to deny, revoke, or suspend specific user accounts. Any student identified as a security risk may be denied access.

In most AUPs, the sanction that is in jeopardy for a violation is the suspension or revocation of the student's Internet account. A standard clause is "The district may suspend the student's access to the district system upon any violation of the AUP."

SAFETY. Districts must be concerned about the safety of students when they have Internet access. In the list of dangers that young people face in today's society, the Internet is clearly not high on the list. Students should be educated on Internet etiquette commonly referred to as netiquette. Netiquette is basically defined as a set of customs that have evolved because they help the Internet work better. Guidelines on the proper utilization of the Internet generally evolve around the use of electronic mail, listservs, newsgroups, or any other electronic means to communicate and infringe on an individual's rights. According to the Talmud, a Jewish commentary on the Bible: "When thou enter a city, abide by its customs." The primary purpose for a set of guidelines (netiquette) is to protect all persons using the Internet

nd those individuals who are not using the Internet but could be affected by
ther persons' usage. Behaviors that should not be permitted on a school
istrict's Internet access include:

- Sharing confidential information on students or employees.
- Sending or displaying offensive messages or pictures.
- Using obscene language.
- Harassing, insulting, or attacking others.
- Engaging in practices that threaten the network.
- Violating copyright laws.
- Using another person's computer password.
- Employing the network for commercial purposes.
- Revealing your name or another person's name and/or personal information.

27

LIABILITY. Districts should also be concerned about the potential that a
ser could violate the district's restriction against purchasing products or
ervices through the system. In the AUP, the district needs to convey clearly
ɔ parents that there is a potential for students to use the system in such a
ɪanner. The district will also want to include in its policy a disclaimer for any
nancial obligations arising from unauthorized use of the system for the
urchase of products or services.

There is potential for a district to be held responsible for losses sustained
ɪy users as a result of a system failure. These losses could involve loss of
ata, interruption of services, or reliance on the accuracy of information
ɪaintained on the district system or accessed through the system. The use of
disclaimer, in an AUP, provides notice of the potential for such loss and
ɪrotects the school district from a liability due to loss of data or any other
ɪatter.

In the Greenfield-Central Community School Corporation policy,
ɔreenfield, Indiana) a statement was included that read:

*The school corporation will not be held liable for: information stored
on school corporation diskettes, hard drives, or servers; information
retrieved through the school corporation computers, networks, or
online resources; personal property used to access school corporation
computers, networks, or online resources; unauthorized financial
obligations resulting from use of school corporation resources and
accounts to access the Internet.*

PRIVACY. Another issue that districts must consider is the privacy
nterest that students or employees may have in the contents of their personal
-mail files. Common phrases in AUPs include:

*All users have the right to privacy in their e-mail. However, if a user is
believed to be in violation of the guidelines stated in this policy, a
system administrator or teacher may need to gain access to private*

correspondence or files. An attempt will be made to notify the user of such inspections whenever possible.

Some AUPs include: "E-mail messages are subject to district review at any time," or "The district can review your personal files at any time."

28

An analogy can be made between student lockers and personal e-mail accounts. Students expect that the district will gain access to lockers on a routine basis for maintenance, but also have a reasonable expectation that the district will generally respect the privacy of their lockers. In practice, there is a strong tendency to treat private e-mail as private, thus, also giving rise to a similar reasonable expectation of privacy.

Finally, it is strongly suggested that the school district's lawyer examine the AUP to see if it is contractual and if the school is being protected from possible liability. Many AUPs have a final statement such as, "Signing this form implies that you agree to all points of the district policy as well as the Acceptable Use Statement." A final statement such as this is an attempt to ensure that all issues, that the district was not able to consider, are (hopefully) covered by some "higher authority," and that all demands or restrictions from that higher authority are also met.

Formulating an AUP

Many different aspects must be considered in formulating an AUP including

- Why is it necessary?
- How is one written?
- What should be included?

NECESSITY FOR AN AUP. AUPs are necessary for several reasons:

- Helping to educate students and parents about the kinds of tools they can use on the network and what they can expect from those tools (in a very general way).
- Helping to define boundaries of behavior, and more critically, to specify the consequences of violating those boundaries.
- Specifying the actions that a system administrator might take in order to maintain or "police" the network — so there are no surprises during the school year.
- Outlining consequences or specific responses to policy violation situations.

WRITING AN AUP. With AUPs being a relatively new concept, many technology coordinators, administrators, and teachers may be unaware of the contents. Most people know that a policy needs to be developed but are not sure of the contents. Time can be saved and schools can benefit from others who have already gone through the process of developing an AUP. The primary question that needs to be addressed is, who should write the AUP? It is important to assign one individual, for example the chair of the business department, the responsibility for selecting a committee to write the policy. As mentioned, earlier policies should be developed with the involvement of teachers, students, administrators, school district technology coordinator(s), parents and/or guardians, and community leaders.

CONTENTS IN AN AUP. All AUPs should explain what the Internet is, how it is used and accessed in the classroom, and what responsibilities the students, parents and/or guardians, and employees have while online. The policy must show how important it is to have the Internet in the classroom. In addition, parents and/or guardians need to be made aware of the potential risks of students obtaining "objectionable" material. This should include definitions for such words as "objectionable."

At a minimum, AUPs should address the use of electronic mail, local technology resources (hardware and software), Internet access, and instructional practice. There are many key points that must be clear and concise in every AUP; they are:

- Explanation of what the Internet is — an electronic highway connecting thousands of computers all over the world and millions of individual subscribers.

- Reasons why access to electronic information resources is being provided.

- Relationship between network access and the district's instructional strategy.

- Responsibilities of school personnel.

- Responsibilities of students.

- Role of parent or guardian.

Access to electronic information and the Internet will enable students to explore thousands of libraries, databases, and bulletin boards, while exchanging messages with Internet users throughout the world. The network is provided for students to conduct research and communicate with others. Electronic information research skills are now fundamental to preparing individuals for future employment and education. Universities are beginning to require knowledge of electronic information resources. All students are expected to know not only what electronic resources are, but how to use them. With any major, including business, liberal arts, or the sciences, the computer and WWW access have become standard in the educational process.

All employees need to learn to use electronic mail and telecommunications tools to be able to apply them daily in performing tasks. Employees are expected to communicate in a professional manner consistent with state laws governing the behavior of school employees and with federal laws governing copyrights. Electronic mail and telecommunications are not to be utilized to share confidential information about students or other employees because messages are not entirely secure. Network administrators may review files and communications to maintain system responsibility. Users should not expect that files stored on a district's computer server will be private.

Privacy in electronic communications is not guaranteed. The school district reserves the right to access stored records, in case there is reasonable cause to suspect wrongdoing or misuse on network systems. Courts have ruled that old messages may be subpoenaed, and network supervisors may examine communications in order to ascertain compliance with network guidelines for acceptable use.

Students are responsible for good behavior on school computer networks just as they are in a classroom or school hallway. Network storage areas may be treated like school lockers. Network administrators may review files and communications to maintain system integrity and ensure that users are using the system responsibly. Access to network services will only be provided to students who agree to act in a considerate and responsible manner.

It is important for school districts to provide disclaimers relating to the buying of products and services via the Internet. An AUP should state that matters involving products and services ordered on the Internet are solely between the seller and the system user.

Ultimately, parents and/or guardians of minors are responsible for setting and conveying the standards that children should follow when using media and information sources. Outside of school, families bear responsibility for such supervision just as they must do with other information sources such as television, telephones, movies, radio, and other media. Parents of students with accounts on the district's system should be aware of the existence of such materials and monitor home usage of the district's system accordingly.

The district assumes no responsibility or liability for any membership or phone charges including, long distance charges, per-minute surcharges, and equipment or line costs incurred by any home usage of the district's system.

Recommendations

It may be prudent for districts to provide recommendations to teachers on the material they select through the Internet for class reading. Teachers should select material that is appropriate in light of the age of students and that is relevant to course objectives. Teachers should preview materials and sites they require or recommend for student access in order to determine the appropriateness of material contained on or accessed through the site. Teachers should provide guidelines and lists of resources to assist students in channeling their research activities effectively and properly when they are accessing the Internet independently. Lastly, teachers should assist students in developing skills to ascertain the truthfulness of information, distinguish fact from opinion, and engage in discussions about controversial issues while demonstrating tolerance and respect for those who hold divergent views.

Clearly, the best way to avoid unnecessary controversy is to place a high priority on providing professional development opportunities for teachers to prepare them to handle this new learning environment. Schools that fail to provide for adequate teacher preparation will be the ones facing the greatest difficulties.

It is very important for all schools that have Internet access to have an AUP. These policies are not something that can be put together quickly. Much time and effort is needed to formulate an AUP. There are many factors to consider, but one of the most important things to understand about these policies is that none are perfect. You will undoubtedly encounter situations that you could not have predicted.

31

Parents need to be reminded that children face more real dangers in their lives than inappropriate exposure to material on the Internet. Children cannot be protected from dangers by erecting barriers but should be given assistance in learning to make appropriate choices. President Clinton stated in his State of the Union Address on February 4, 1997:

> . . . As the Internet becomes our new town square, a computer in every home — a teacher of all subjects, a connection to all cultures — this will no longer be a dream, but a necessity.

As we prepare for the millennium, we need to prepare students to utilize the Internet as an educational tool to further enhance their knowledge and skills.

References

Acceptable Use Policy Greenfield-Central High School. [Online]. Available: http://gcsc.k12.in.us/AUP/AUP.html.

Bellingham Public Schools. [Online]. Available: http://www.bham.wednet.edu/2313proc.html.

Gresham-Barlow School District. [Online]. Available: http://www.gresham.k12.or.us/aubHBGA-AR-1.html.

Los Angeles Unified School District Information Technology Division. [Online]. Available: http://lausd.k12.us/aup.html.

Internet Applications Related to National Standards for Business Education

Chapter 4 — Career Development

by Nancy D. Zeliff
Northwest Missouri State University — Maryville, Missouri

School-to-Work, Tech Prep, preparing students for and about business, these have been initiatives of business education. Of course, in simple terms, these career development initiatives prepare today's students to be tomorrow's workers. Career development begins in preschool and elementary school with career awareness, continues in middle school through aptitudinal and attitudinal assessment, and culminates formal education with the job search process.

The Internet can provide information at all phases of career development — very current and authentic information. The Worldwide Web (WWW) allows students to discover career options, read about companies, locate job vacancies, prepare a resume, post an electronic resume, and simulate an interview. Traditional career development procedures and methods remain, but indeed new ones are being employed.

Career Development

Career development is the "process by which a student develops his or her self-concept, explores career options, and acquires skills and information that will help him or her make decisions about the future" (Smith and Edmunds, 1995, p. 11). The phases by which career development is delivered are career awareness, career orientation, career exploration, career preparation, and career specialization (*School-to-Work Transition*, 1994).

CAREER AWARENESS. Career awareness begins in the early school years. Activities bring an awareness of different careers before students.

CAREER ORIENTATION. During elementary and middle school years, students participate in activities that orient them to different careers.

CAREER EXPLORATION. Possible career goals are selected in the middle school years when students explore career paths.

CAREER PATHS. Career paths are "clusters of occupations/careers that are grouped because the people in them share similar interests and strengths" (*Exploring Career Paths*, 1994, p. 3). Many occupations are listed within a career path that offer students an area in which to focus research and attention. At the same time, each path offers flexibility and a variety of options to pursue. Career paths offer a concentration for students which leads to school courses taken, job shadowing completed, and class projects chosen — all reflective of a selected career path.

The six career paths available are: arts and communication; business, management, and technology; health services; human services/transportation; industrial and engineering technology; and natural resources/agriculture (*Exploring Career Paths*, 1994).

CAREER PREPARATION. In high school, occupational skills and supervised work experience can be combined to allow students to prepare for a chosen career. Options for career advancement and postsecondary education are also investigated in this phase.

CAREER SPECIALIZATION. An upgrade of skills or development of new skills is pursued in this phase. The need for lifelong learning and mastery of new career-specific skills will become evident to the worker.

Career Activities

Depending on the phase of career development, a variety of simulated or authentic activities are available. Print materials, audiovisual media, speakers, field trips, career aptitude and interest assessments, job shadowing, supervised work experiences, career portfolios, and apprenticeship are opportunities by which prospective workers progress through all phases of career development. The Internet now offers the means to implement these activities.

Sources of Information

Career development is most successful when a mix of traditional and innovative approaches are used. Personal networking among family and friends is still highly successful. The classified section of newspapers and employment agencies still yield job prospects. Career and job fairs still connect job candidates with employers. However, today's innovative resources available on the Internet bring a wealth of current strategies and information to individuals involved in career development.

PRINT MATERIALS. Varied print sources of information are available. Governmental agencies, professional organizations, labor unions, companies, and authored books are appropriate sources of career information.

Finkelstein (1995) lists suggested reading for job candidates or individuals changing careers to include:

- *What Color is Your Parachute?* by Richard N. Bolles.
- *Making Vocational Choices: A Theory of Careers* by John L. Holland.
- *Transitions — Making Sense of Life's Changes* by William Bridges.
- *Passages* by Gail Sheehy.
- *Who's Hiring Who?* by Richard Lathrop.
- *Dictionary of Occupational Titles* by the U.S. Department of Labor.
- *Moving Up* by Eli Djeddah.

INTERNET. The Internet now offers a means by which career activities an be completed and information collected from varied electronic sources. he WWW, the most popular medium of the Internet, offers three advantages ɔ individuals involved in career development.

The WWW is convenient, flexible, and cost-effective (*StudentCenter*, 997). Individuals can access information on the WWW at any time and on ny day. With keyword searches through databases and search engines, a pecific region or specific job can be identified. The links from one site to nother bring a wealth of information to the searcher — all in a very cost-ffective manner. Outside of initial computer hardware, software, and ietwork costs, the job search can cost "nothing." Some services are fee-ased, however, dependent on information received and services rendered.

Some of the useful information on career development available on the VWW includes:

- Business sites with company information, job opportunities, financial information, annual reports, and contact names available.
- Government and professional organizations/labor union sites listing industry information, trends, and compensation.
- Employment guides from nonprofit and proprietary sources.
- Electronic job sites from proprietary organizations, daily newspapers, and public and private employment agencies.
- College and university career centers with lists of job opportunities, internships, job search techniques, online resume databases, and online registration of job candidates.
- Regional and community sites with state, county, or city information (*StudentCenter,* 1997).

The WWW is not the only Internet tool helpful in career development. Networking with individuals in selected occupations through newsgroups, mailing sts, and e-mail is also available. This "electronic mentoring" is a service available rom professional organizations or through Internet communications.

Steps to the Right Job

A model helpful for individuals in the career preparation and pecialization phases of career development is the *Career Development Manual*

(University of Waterloo, 1997). The steps involved in career preparation and specialization are self-assessment, occupational research, decision-making, employer contact, and the job.

SELF-ASSESSMENT. In this process, the individual assesses his or her personality traits, skills, knowledge, interests and values, and achievements. Vocational, aptitude, attitude, and personality assessments are available. Feedback from these assessments help individuals identify possible skills and characteristics of certain occupations and careers that would be suitable or not suitable.

OCCUPATIONAL RESEARCH. Personal experience through interviews, job shadowing, supervised work experience, internships, apprenticeships, and literature review provides information about occupations. Trends, projected openings, duties and tasks performed, and compensation for respective career paths and their occupations are presented.

DECISION-MAKING. Information now available is reviewed and analyzed. Feedback from varied self-assessment strategies and information received from occupational research allow one to establish a career goal, seek out needed training, locate a training or educational institution, and plan a time frame in which to prepare for the chosen occupation.

EMPLOYER CONTACT. The job search identifies existing job vacancies. When a specific vacancy is located, one follows with writing an application letter and resume, completing a job application form, interviewing, and writing follow-up correspondence.

THE JOB. Finally, a job offer is made to the applicant, and an acceptance letter is written. These steps in career preparation and specialization no longer must be completed with traditional means of print resources and human networking. Again, the electronic tools on the Internet provide current, convenient, flexible, and cost-effective information to complete the steps to the right job.

Case Study #1

Marty is a ninth grade student who has chosen the business, management, and technology career path. Marty is interested especially in technology and personal computers. Follow Marty with the implementation of the Internet to investigate this chosen career path.

SELF-ASSESSMENT. Assessment strategies are available in print that an individual can complete to assess talents, interests, and personal, physical, and mental characteristics. These assessments, once taken with pen and paper at career centers or with guidance counselors, can be taken interactively on the WWW.

Career Safari (*Tripod*, 1997) links to two career aptitude personality profiles. Marty took a personal profile test online and received a profile via e-mail on dislikes, likes, and preferences. Also completed online was the Keirsey Temperament Sorter which brought immediate responses back hrough the WWW browser. Both assessments are based on the Myers-Briggs 'ersonality Profile. The Career Interests Game©, based on Holland's career heories, is also available online (University of Missouri-Columbia, 1997, and 3all State University, 1997).

Feedback to Marty indicates strong interests in technology and above verage aptitude in computer technologies. Therefore, Marty continues in the :areer path of business, management, and technology.

OCCUPATIONAL RESEARCH. Today's workplace is different from that of an earlier generation. New management styles, current technologies, :lobal competition, and diversity are present in the workplace. Workers need :ommunication, problem-solving, and decision-making skills (ERIC 171, .996). Jobs in the goods-producing sector are not as common as the services-)roducing sector.

Marty locates several career sites on the WWW which provide informa- ion about high growth jobs. Retail sales, health care, robotics, computer :raphics, telecommunications, and biotechnology are industries with high job)pportunities (*TheStar*, 1997). Paralegals, chefs, public relations managers, ravel agents, management consultants, health services administrators,)sychologists, computer scientists, systems analysts, human service workers, ind actuaries are occupations with expected growth in the 21st century.

Marty accesses career profiles via the WWW published by the Bureau of .abor Statistics. These profiles describe job duties and tasks, training and :ducation needed, and expected compensation (*Tripod*, 1997). A wealth of)ccupational information is found in the *Occupational Outlook Handbook* 1996), also available online. Marty is excited to see that computer occupa- ions are among the high growth jobs.

Marty also researches leading information technology companies to <now what they expect from employees, to read job descriptions in computer- 'elated positions, and to establish an expected entry-level salary. The *Fortune* 500 company listing, Dun and Bradstreet business background report, EDGAR J.S. Securities and Exchange Commissions' database of corporate informa- ion, and JobTrak's Company Profiles are helpful in researching companies Ball State University, 1997).

From the career information, Marty realizes that at least two years of)ostsecondary education is needed for computer-related jobs. Extensive nformation on educational institutions is available from The Education and :areer Center (Petersons, 1997). Information on colleges and universities, 'ocational-technical centers, distance learning, and financial assistance is vailable at this site.

DECISION-MAKING. From this occupational, educational, and company nformation, Marty now develops a career plan with input from parents, :eachers, and guidance counselors. This career plan lists interests and apti- udes discovered from the self-assessment phase. Four high growth occupa- ions are listed from the business, management, and technology career path.

Marty will concentrate his career plan in the occupational areas of robotics, computer graphics, telecommunications, and systems analysis.

High school courses needed to prepare for postsecondary work are planned, postsecondary educational requirements and possible institutions are identified, high school activities helpful for this career path are listed, and personal experiences and future part-time jobs relative to computer technologies are discussed. Marty's career plan has evolved with the Internet as the source of reference and information.

38

Case Study #2

Chris is in the last semester of a computer graphics program at a postsecondary institution. Using the Internet, Chris undertakes the job search process and visits the career center on campus.

Colleges and universities are beginning to utilize the WWW as a medium by which available jobs are listed and job candidates' resumes and information are stored within databases. Seniors and alumni at Northwest Missouri State University register with the Office of Career Services through a personal identification number (PIN). Electronic resumes can also be constructed (Northwest, 1997). When an employer requests a list of qualified candidates with a particular major, Career Services queries the online database and generates a list of candidates and prints their electronic resumes. Registered seniors and alumni can access a list of job vacancies through the Career Services WWW home page (Martin, 1997).

Use of the Internet should not be Chris' only means for job information. Electronically oriented and "progressive" companies may be comfortable with career centers utilizing the WWW. However, traditional means of registering job vacancies and candidates may be necessary until the WWW and Internet access is completely universal. Job candidates are advised to be cautious in listing personal information such as phone numbers and social security numbers on electronic resumes (ERIC 172, 1996).

EMPLOYER CONTACT. Chris seeks out the various online job banks available to see what computer graphics jobs are available in a preferred geographic region. Campus career centers with WWW home pages have links to these varied sources. Services of these online job banks are usually free, but some are fee-based. Services offered include employment opportunities by countries or regions of the United States, a resume database, electronic resume construction, and job search tips on interviews, resumes, and application letters. Chris locates a computer graphics position to pursue. The "Big Six Job Databases" (CNET, 1997) are:

- Online Career Center
- CareerMosaic
- E-Span
- The Monster Board

- Career Magazine
- America's Job Bank

APPLICATION LETTER. Four types of application letters are discussed on JobTrak's (1997) site and include examples of standard, targeted, unsolicited/resume, and networking letters. Chris chooses to write a targeted application letter which clearly specifies skills and qualifications needed for the specific computer graphics position.

39

RESUME. Chris reviews resume styles, design guidelines, and format techniques on numerous WWW sites on resume writing. Syndicated columnists and noted authors have WWW sites on resume construction.

Four resume styles are highlighted on the Kaplan Career Center (1996) site. The chronological or most traditional style is a reverse chronological listing of career highlights and draws attention to experience in one profession or with prestigious employers. The *functional* style emphasizes abilities and skills of the job candidate and reduces the importance of work history. Entry-level candidates with little experience or individuals changing careers are best served with this style of resume. The *targeted* resume, like the targeted application letter, lists specific skills and qualifications for a specific job. Chris chooses to complement the targeted application letter with a targeted resume because of experience in college with computer graphics, desktop publishing, and WWW page design. The *broadcast* resume or *bio* is an experimental style. This is a letter describing the job candidate and used in unsolicited requests for informational interviews (Kaplan, 1996). A *vita*, a fifth resume style, is used predominantly in education or among job candidates who have a long history in a particular occupation or industry and who are applying for a similar occupation or within the same industry.

Because Chris has chosen a targeted resume that will list specific skills and qualifications for the computer graphics position, categories on the resume may include Computer Skills, Computer Graphics Projects, and Communication Skills. These categories would clearly highlight Chris' qualifications and competence in these areas and how they match those of the position. In other styles of resumes, more common categories are:

- Career Objective
- Education
- Related Work Experience
- Other Work Experience
- Honors and Awards
- References

The use of keywords is especially important with a targeted resume but also advisable with the use of resume scanning software. These words and phrases convey specific skills and accomplishments (JobTrak, 1997). Because computers are not proficient at picking out the action verbs used in traditional resumes, keywords should be nouns. Some examples of these words are:

- Financial Analysis
- Windows 95
- Communication Skills
- Leadership

- Excel
- Sales
- Accountant
- Team Player

Resume scanning is becoming the major way companies screen applicants (Besson, 1997). This process involves a computer that scans a resume as an image, not text. Next, optical character recognition (OCR) software scans the image to create a text file in ASCII that the computer understands. "Artificial intelligence reads the scanned text and extracts such information" (Besson, 1997, p. 1) about a job candidate. The software programs seek out keywords that match specific job qualifications and can only identify certain type styles, sizes, and formats. Therefore, the use of bolding, italics, graphic lines, and unusual fonts is not advised. Chris reads online information regarding the use of keywords for targeted resumes and the strong possibility the submitted resume will be scanned. Keywords are used and traditional fonts and type styles are selected for Chris' resume.

Resumix, Inc. (1997) offers these additional tips for constructing scannable resumes.

- Use white or light colored 8-1/2 x 11 paper, printed on one side only.
- Submit a laser printed copy.
- Use standard typefaces such as Helvetica, Times, and New Century Schoolbook.
- Use a 10, 12, or 14 point size font.
- Use bolding and all uppercase letters in headings only.
- Avoid bolding, italics, shadows, and underlining in text.
- Avoid horizontal lines and two column resume formats.
- List each phone number on a separate line.

Chris locates two WWW sites that have resume assessment checklists. An interactive checklist assesses basic resume writing (Kendall, 1996). JobTrak's (1997) site allows for a candidate to check off resume components and concepts used successfully.

JobTrak (1997) suggests job candidates prepare three resumes — a mail version, scannable version, and an Internet version. A mail version is printed on high quality bond paper with design elements of bullets, italics, and other visual effects. A scannable version is word processed but uses keywords and phrases. No visual effects are present that would affect the acceptance" of a candidate by the computer software. A third version — he Internet resume — is a plain text document that is sent through e-mail.

Posting a resume on the WWW is a fourth resume option for job candidates. Several sites offer this service — free or fee-based. Templates are available that job candidates complete through interactive forms on the WWW. These posted resumes can then be accessed by employers subscribing to the service. Chris opts for all four versions of resume dissemination. However, Chris takes into consideration JobTrak's (1997) points to posting a resume online:

- Do not list home addresses and home phone numbers. Lease a voice mail service or post office box to ensure privacy.
- Check the confidentiality of the database or resume service.
- Verify the posted resume can be updated at no charge.
- Confirm the "life" of the posted resume. When will it be deleted?

INTERVIEW. Chris has progressed through the first two stages of the job search and is now slated to complete an on-site interview for the computer graphics position. The WWW offers numerous sites for preparing for the job interview.

Varied types of interviews include *preliminary interviews* at college career centers, career fairs, and those arranged through networking. *Phone interviews* are initiated by the employer, often to screen candidates or when a face-to-face interview is not possible. *On-site interviews* bring the candidate to the company for a more extensive visit, tour, and interview(s) (Ball State University, 1997). *Behavioral interviews* are being adopted by more companies. The premise of these interviews is that past behavior of the job candidate is the best predictor for future success.

Therefore, questions are asked of the candidate that call for specific examples of past experiences (Stimac, 1995). Sample questions are:

- Give me a specific example of when you worked among diversity. What was difficult about the situation? What was an easy transition?
- Cite an example of working with a difficult person. How did you turn this negative situation into a positive situation?

JobTrak (1997) lists five different interview styles. Chris prepares in anticipation that interviews take on different forms and can be conducted by more than one interviewer.

Directed interviews have a definite structure based on a list of prepared questions. Nondirected interviews are less structured and based on broader questions asked by the interviewer. Nonverbally, the applicant is encouraged to present qualifications. Stress interviews are not commonly used, but their purpose is to place the job candidate under pressure to test reaction and decision-making. Group interviews are when more than one candidate is interviewed at once and are used to determine how candidates interact as team members. Stress and group interviews are commonly used in leadership academies that license or grant certification. Panel interviews involve one job candidate and more than one interviewer (JobTrak, 1997).

Chris locates many sites that list questions often asked of job candidates. Suitable answers are provided as well as questions candidates should ask of employers. Interview guidelines and tips are also available on the WWW. Finkelstein (1995) suggests the following interviewing tips:

- Know about the organization.

- Present oneself positively.
- Dress appropriately.
- Do not smoke.
- Be assertive.
- Start high in terms of salary but be willing to negotiate.

Also in preparation for the interview, Chris practices with an interactive mock interview on the WWW. Responses are evaluated and ranked according to their appropriateness. An index is awarded to the interviewee to measure successful interviewing techniques (Kaplan, 1996).

EMPLOYMENT PORTFOLIO. Through Chris' computer graphics classes, projects were completed, programs written, and WWW pages designed. Chris has compiled these artifacts and placed them in a professional employment portfolio. Suggestions for compiling the portfolio that will be taken to on-site interviews are available online. Benefits of using an employment portfolio are:

- The employment portfolio sets job candidates apart from each other.
- The items in the portfolio can show evidence of competence in job skills.
- The portfolio items are supportive documents to be used in the interview (Ball State University, 1997).

INTERVIEW FOLLOW-UP. After returning from the interview, Chris follows up with letters thanking the organization and interviewer(s) for the opportunity to interview. If the position is offered to Chris, an acceptance or denial letter must also be written. Chris found WWW sites with sample letters and guidelines for construction (Ball State University, 1997).

Summary

The Internet can serve as a complete source of career development information and activities. Coupled with traditional methods of human networking, print media, and employment agencies, individuals involved in career development have a broader and more current scope of information and resources. Because of the dynamic environment of the Internet, WWW sites can change frequently and unpredictably. This is, however, an advantage in that current information can be maintained and listed.

Preparing today's students to be tomorrow's workers through School-to-Work, Tech Prep, classes *for* and *about* business, and other career development initiatives is now dynamic and self-initiated with the convenience, flexibility, and cost-effectiveness of the Internet.

References

Ball State University. Career Services. [Online]. Available: http://www.bsu.edu/careers/.

Besson, T. (1997). Why a "Scannable" Version of Your Resume Is a Must. *National Business Employment Weekly*. [Online]. Available: http://www.cweb.com/cw/NBEW.besson.htm.

CNET. The Big Six Job Databases. [Online]. Available: http://www.cnet.com/Content/Features/Net/Jobs/database.html.

ERIC 171. (1996). Job Training Versus Career Development: What Is Voc Ed's Role? ERIC Digest No. 171. Columbus, OH: Center on Education and Training for Employment.

ERIC 172. (1996). Wired: The Electronic Job Search. ERIC Digest No. 172. Columbus, OH: Center on Education and Training for Employment.

Exploring Career Paths: A Guide for Students and Their Families. (1994). Columbia, MO: Instructional Materials Laboratory.

Finkelstein, K. A Career and Resume Guide. [Online]. Available: http://digiscape.com/career/jobhome.htm.

JobTrak. Cover Letters/Application Letters. [Online]. Available: http://www.jobtrak.com/jobsearch_docs/.

Kaplan. Career Center. [Online]. Available: http://www.kaplan.com/career/.

Kendall, P. Do-It-Yourself Resume Assessment. [Online]. Available: http://www.connectme.com/advice/resume/assessmnt.html.

Martin, L. (1997, February). Interview in Office of Career Services. Maryville, MO: Northwest Missouri State University.

Northwest Missouri State University. Office of Career Services. [Online]. Available: http://198.209.246.112/.

Occupational Outlook Handbook. [Online]. Available: http://stats.bls.gov/ocohome.htm.

Petersons. The Education and Career Center. [Online]. Available: http://www.petersons.com.

Resumix, Inc. Preparing the Ideal Scannable Resume. [Online]. Available: http://www.resumix.com/resume/resume_tips.html.

School-to-Work Transition: An Introduction to Georgia's Career Development Initiative. (1994). Atlanta: Georgia Department of Education.

Smith, C. L. and Edmunds, N. A. (1995). *The Vocational Instructor's Survival Guide*. Alexandria, VA: The American Vocational Association.

Stimac, D. J. Behavioral Interviews — A Job Candidate's Toughest Obstacle. [Online]. Available: http://www.careermag.com/newsarts/interviewing/1050.html.

StudentCenter. Who am I? Using the Web to Succeed in Your Job Search. [Online]. Available: http://studentcenter.com/who/interjob/interjob.htm.

TheStar. Top Jobs for the Next Century. [Online]. Available: http://kcstar.webpoint.com/jobtop_jobs.htm.

Tripod. Tripod's Career Safari. [Online]. Available: http://www.tripod.com/work/safari/.

University of Missouri-Columbia. Career Center: The Career Interests Game© [Online]. Available: http://www.missouri.edu.

University of Waterloo. Career Development Manual. [Online]. Available: http://www.adm.uwaterloo.ca/infocecs/CRC/manual-home.html.

43

Chapter 5 — Basic Business and Personal Finance

by Jim Mansfield
University of Missouri-St. Louis — St. Louis, Missouri
and
Lonnie Echternacht
University of Missouri-Columbia — Columbia, Missouri

The Information Superhighway is expanding rapidly, connecting schools, businesses, government agencies, and individuals to an enormous variety of resources stored on computers around the world. Much of this information is applicable for use in basic business and personal finance courses, and accessing it is easier than one might think. Once connected to the Internet, users can obtain and share information with millions of individuals throughout the nation and even the world.

Many of the technological advancements that have occurred are impacting our daily lives. Suddenly, televisions have over 200 channels and are used as computer screens. We pay income taxes to the United States Government electronically for quicker refunds. Bank ATMs provide access to cash 24 hours a day, and paychecks are electronically deposited in bank accounts. Just as quickly, money for utility bills, mortgage payments, and insurance premiums are withdrawn from bank accounts via telephone lines.

The world is changing very rapidly. In the 1950s, only a few select businesses used computers. In the 1970s, approximately 50,000 computers existed worldwide. Today, approximately 50,000 computers are manufactured on a daily basis. Shopping can now be done from home networks on our television sets which never close. Software can be purchased and installed on home PCs, which allow us to do financial planning and simplify saving and investing for retirement years. Telephones now are cellular and can be used to make phone calls while traveling in airplanes several miles above the ground. We now hear telephone enhancement services such as conference calls, redial, caller ID, and call forwarding being used every day. In fact, e-mail addresses and Web sites are becoming more common in the business world than home addresses and telephone numbers.

Students are acquiring a computer knowledge base much more sophisticated than we had ever dreamed. They use highly interactive games, Web sites, and e-mail simply by keying in a few strokes on an electronic keyboard or clicking a mouse. Schools must incorporate today's technology into their instructional programs and use whatever is available to enhance students' learning. We must change our concepts of teaching and learning in much the same way we have changed our telephone procedures and banking activities. Technology and the Internet have four practical applications within the school classroom: as an independent subject, as a teaching assistant, as a tool for instruction, and finally as means of transforming the process of learning. Table 1 lists the differences between a traditional basic business and personal finance classroom and an interactive classroom that uses the Internet.

The following nine basic business and personal finance subject areas are correlated with the National Business Education Association's (NBEA) *National Standards for Business Education*. Suggested Internet classroom activities and a major instructional/learning project are provided for each of the subject areas.

Banking

Financial institutions provide a variety of money-related services to individuals. While banks still serve as multipurpose financial centers to numerous people, many of these services are also provided by other financial institutions such as savings and loans, credit unions, credit card companies, finance companies, and retail stores.

The Internet provides many excellent opportunities for students to visit financial institutions' Web sites and acquire or download information pertinent to the following:

- Compare the different basic services provided by local banks and other financial institutions.
- Examine the role of the Federal Reserve System and the banking system in the United States.
- Describe the functions of banks and other financial institutions in the United States economy.
- Compile data relative to actual interest rates being paid and charged by different financial institutions.
- Convert dollars to other currencies such as yens, pounds, or deutschmarks by using an online currency converter.
- Compare the use of bank debit cards, including electronic transfer of funds, with standard consumer credit cards.

Students can examine ways to conduct banking transactions from home by using a computer, a commercial software program such as Quicken or BankNow, and the Internet. In addition, search engines can be used to display a list of banks offering online banking. Using Web sites to obtain information, students can compile the benefits and costs of electronic

Table 1: A Comparison of Lesson Planning — Traditional vs. Using the Internet

Traditional Basic Business and Personal Finance Classrooms	VS.	Interactive Basic Business and Personal Finance Classrooms Using the Internet
Teacher provides information from a textbook and leads discussion of major topic areas.		Information comes from a variety of electronic sources in response to major topic areas.
Students take notes and retrieve printed information on demand.		Students create, share, discuss, and use information to solve problems by exchanging e-mail, browsing the Web, and using search engines.
Teacher, textbook, school library, and local resources are available to students.		Students also have access to global resources including the Internet, ERIC, and CD-ROM technology.
Students are expected to master information presented by the teacher.		Students are expected to use electronic technology to compile and analyze information to solve authentic classroom tasks.
Students solve classroom directed activities which illustrate basic textbook concepts.		Students solve real world problems with up-to-date relevant information obtained from a variety of sources.
Curriculum is shaped by logical progression through content area materials and the textbook.		Curriculum is shaped by the user's own needs and knowledge required to solve authentic tasks.
Evaluation is based on textbook-related and/or teacher-constructed tests.		Evaluation is based on portfolios and student performance as well as self and teacher assessment.
Teacher is the authority and major source of knowledge for all classroom activities.		Teacher is a mentor and guides classroom activities, facilitates learning, and often learns the material along with the students.

banking. The typical benefits identified should include, but are not limited to, convenience, speed, readily available account balances, online help, and the ability to download bank statements on demand. Typical costs of electronic banking that students will identify are the bank monthly service charge, software, minimum deposit required, and Internet access charges.

Saving and Investing

People often talk about the importance of putting money aside for a "rainy day." In today's society with increasing costs of education, housing, medical care, food, and transportation, is it possible to save? Is it worth the sacrifice? Banks, savings and loans, mutual savings banks, credit unions, and stockbrokers offer many opportunities for the average person to invest and save for retirement at the same time. Items typically offered include: certificates of deposit, government and municipal bonds, individual retirement accounts (IRAs), stocks and bonds, mutual funds, and profit sharing plans. Each of these items, which are not covered by the Federal Deposit Insurance Corporation (FDIC), carries a potential risk of losing all or part of the total investment.

The Internet provides numerous sources of information helpful in making investment decisions. Students are able to find online a wide range of resources concerning investments by using keyword searches and Web browsing techniques. Some good starting points are: online publications such as *Mutual Funds Magazine, Business Week, Fortune, The Wall Street Journal, Money,* and *Investing Update*; financial databases including Hoover's Online, the Securities and Exchange Commission's EDGAR (Electronics Data Gathering, Analysis, and Retrieval) System, Access Business Online, and Onramp Access, Inc.; and individual Web sites of investment companies. The wide range of resources available on the Internet helps students integrate information and engage in learning activities that will enable them to:

- Compile a list of reasons why and how people save.

- Compare the rate of return of mutual finds with other investment options such as individual stocks and bonds, certificates of deposit, and savings accounts.

- Analyze the factors that affect the rate of return on a given savings or investment plan incorporating actual examples (e.g., current return, rate of risk, and liquidity).

- Differentiate between interest, dividends, capital gains, and rent from property using real world examples.

- Explain why a savings and investment plan changes as one grows older.

- Describe how individuals' savings and investing activities influence capital formation and economic growth.

An excellent savings and investing class project is an in-depth study of the stock market using the Internet. A simulated purchase of an equal amount of stocks, mutual funds, and certificates of deposits (CDs) could be monitored for different time periods. Students may find different rates of return for 30, 60, and 120-day time periods. Using the Web provides a comprehensive view of market activity. Exploring individual company Web sites, accessing pertinent data, and integrating that information into a spreadsheet or word processing document to justify individual and/or group investment decisions enrich this class project. Students should prepare graphs and charts depicting their individual investment results and also check the Internet or overall market trends during the same time period. Answers to pertinent questions and up-to-date relevant information can be obtained easily and quickly by students who use e-mail and FTP. Composing, sending, receiving, replying to, and forwarding e-mail messages are important business skills for today's youth. Competition among individual students or groups of students for the largest gain on investment or the best presentation of actual documentation supporting their investment decisions generates enthusiasm for the activity and increases student learning.

49

Shopping Decisions

Helping today's students acquire the skills needed to survive and prosper in today's complex marketplace is critical. Developing in-depth thinking skills—that include comparing, analyzing, inferring, and evaluating—and using decision-making skills to examine consumer problems and practice wise consumer shopping are important life skills. In addition, the influence of marketing and advertising techniques on consumer demand needs to be explored.

Commercial activity on the Web is increasing daily. Many vendors maintain sites on the World Wide Web (WWW) that provide product information, phone numbers, and e-mail addresses that can be used to place orders. Also, Web sites that resemble "online shopping malls" provide links to a variety of different companies' products and services. A growing number of individuals as well as businesses use the Internet to purchase goods and services and to get online customer service and product support from vendors.

Students can access a rich depository of resource materials on the Internet that relate to shopping decisions and allow them to:

- Identify major companies promoting their products on the Web and choose one of the companies to explore in depth.

- Determine the types of businesses that locate in an online mall.

- Compare product presentations and costs of an online mall with local or nearby shopping malls and/or catalogs.

- Assess the influence of the "glamour" of the Web page on purchasing decisions.

- Discuss how students would prefer to do their shopping. Where would their parents prefer to shop?

- Identify factors that influence product consumption and service after the sale.

- Compare online advertisements to actual product specifications and performance.

Students should access the Internet Advertising Resource Guide, which has links to selected sources of information about advertising and marketing on the Internet. The guide's primary thrust is education; and uniqueness, usefulness, and depth of information are the criteria used for inclusion. The main sections of the guide include Internet Marketing, Advertising, Prices, Internet Marketing/Advertising, Research and Teaching, Associations' Web Pages, Advertising Departments' Web Pages, Doing Business on the Internet, and Exemplary Commercial Storefronts. Students can access product or vendor support information, as well as learn about companies and their products and services by examining Web sites. For example, students should be expected to use search engines to locate Web sites that provide both company and product information as well as product and customer support.

50

Credit

Credit usage has been a way of life for most consumers in the past few decades. "Buy now, pay later," is the philosophy of many Americans. Credit allows the immediate use of products or services in exchange for a promise to pay in the future. The use of credit creates a debt, but people generally find the term "credit" more acceptable than the term "debt." Goods and services can be purchased and paid for online on the Internet using either a secured or unsecured credit card transaction, a company that approves and collects for purchases, or "e-cash or cyber money."

Numerous credit resources can be located on the Internet by using keyword searches and browsing Web sites. A comparative analysis of shopping for products and services on the WWW with traditional credit purchases enables students to:

- Summarize the provisions of major credit laws.
- Describe the major risks associated with credit card purchases on the Internet.
- Identify the types of credit card misuse/fraud resulting from Internet transactions.
- Check and see how many consumer rights agencies are listed on the Internet; and what kinds of help they are willing to provide.
- Compile the disadvantages of using a credit card for major purchases.
- Explain why banks charge different rates of interest for different types of loans.
- Analyze why some credit card companies charge an annual fee for their cards and why some do not.

A credit-related Internet project to determine the total cost of a major purchase that has payments divided equally over 36 months and 60 months is an "eye-opener" for students. For example, students could compare the final cost of financing a new car with a large down payment versus a "zero down, $99 a month" transaction. The lowest interest rate available should be determined by checking the Web sites of banks, credit card companies, and other appropriate lending agencies. Students are expected to present a comparison of the costs of the credit purchase by displaying actual information from at least three different sources of credit.

Financial Resources and Budgeting

Why are some people able to reach their saving goals and others are living from "week to week"? The answer could be "living within one's means." A personal budget which includes a road map to guide an individual's spending and savings activities is the answer. The personal budget should be realistic, reflect one's material needs and wants, and be carefully thought through.

The Internet provides a wealth of information concerning financial resources that help in the development of workable budgets. Suggestions for students' use of the Internet to research budgeting information quickly and enhance their learning include:

- Compare the costs of two different automobiles. Which automobile costs the most and why?

- Compare the price of several household items offered for sale on different Web sites. Be sure similar items are used for comparison purposes.

- Have students prepare a personal budget using the Internet. Some expense categories could be predetermined for students. Students that finish early or have online access can be encouraged to add additional items to their budgets or supply greater detail.

- Examples of actual student budgets could be placed on the course home page for students to review and critique easily.

Successful budgets require a vast amount of planning. The Internet provides generic budgets which can be adapted to fit one's own lifestyle. An interesting credit-related Internet project is to work online with financial planning software, available through several different Web sites, and prepare a budget for one's current family. If possible, the budget should include the actual family income and address housing, utilities, groceries, car expenses, miscellaneous expenses, medical and health insurance costs, and savings. The budget generated by the financial planning software can then be compared to the family's actual expenditures to analyze how the family can improve its spending and saving of financial resources.

Protecting Against Risks

Managing personal risks to improve the likelihood of protecting assets and income against loss is risk management. Risk management is a three-step process: identifying risks, assessing risks, and handling risks. To handle a risk, an individual may choose to insure against, avoid, reduce, or assume the risk.

Some collaborative Internet activities are presented below to enhance both the teaching and learning of protecting (insuring) against risks. Students are expected to work in groups and access insurance company as well as other financially oriented Web sites to:

- Determine ways to obtain protection against the consequences of various risks.

- Explain the purpose and types of life insurance and property insurance coverages.

- Compare the coverages and costs associated with private and group health insurance policies.

- Analyze why some groups of drivers have to pay higher auto insurance rates and identify some of the higher-paying groups.

- Compare the rates of different auto insurance companies for the same kinds of coverage on different types of automobiles.

- Identify various public and private suppliers of insurance.

- Explain why insurance needs change throughout one's life.

- Explore the litigation costs of companies and individuals even when they win.

- Compare the procedures necessary for filing claims with two major insurance companies.

While the following instructional/learning activity (Weston, 1996) can be adapted to many different business courses, it particularly lends itself to the study of insurance. The Internet is a valuable tool for looking up quickly the meaning of acronyms related to the topic or unit being studied. The insurance learning activity may progress as follows:

- Each student draws an acronym out of a "hat." A sample list of insurance acronyms might include: IRA, FICA, TIAA CREF, POS, HMO, VALIC, FDIC, and AARP.

- Students may use the following Internet site to search for the words represented by their particular acronyms: http://curia.ucc.ie/egi-gin/acronym.

- Students record the words. If there is more than one meaning for the acronym, all possibilities should be noted. For verification that they actually located the Web site, students are also expected to record the acronyms that come immediately before and immediately after theirs.

- Students are then expected to search on the WWW for information about their respective acronyms; each student prepares at least a paragraph explaining the meaning and use of the acronym.

- Students e-mail the instructor with the results of their searches, keeping in mind acceptable netiquette when they communicate electronically.

axes

The average person works about five months a year to pay taxes levied y various governmental agencies as well as federal, state, county, and city xes. The amount of taxes paid depends to a great extent on where one ves, what one earns, what one buys, and what one owns. Taxes are the rices paid for services. Taxes provide for services such as schools, police and re protection, mass transportation, national defense, social security, and relfare. The federal government is the largest spender of our tax dollars. It is nportant for students to understand the different taxes individuals pay and ie benefits they receive.

A wealth of Internet resources is available to help students strengthen ieir understanding of taxes. Sample instructional/learning Internet activities elated to taxes are:

- Assume a salary for a family of four living in two different states. Which state requires the higher payroll taxes?

- Compare the sales tax rates of those states that have a state income tax with those states that do not.

- Assume an individual owns a house valued at $134,000. Figure the amount of property taxes that would be owed annually if the house was located in each of the following cities: St. Louis, Des Moines, Los Angeles, Dallas, Boston, Miami, and your home town.

A suggested Internet class project for the study of taxes requires that tudents work together online with the Internal Revenue Service (IRS) to ccess the necessary tax forms for filing federal income taxes. Students are xpected to use specific teacher-provided information concerning salary, leductions, withholdings, and number of dependents and then work online to igure income taxes owed. An expanded assignment would be to assign each roup three different states and have them use the above information to letermine if federal and state income taxes differ from state to state.

onsumer Rights and Responsibilities

The United States economy operates as a free enterprise system. Supply nd demand are key factors that determine what products or services are roduced, in what quantity, and at what price. The marketplace is full of leceptive and misleading ways suppliers increase demand for their products. onsumers must be aware of the following ways that advertisers mislead onsumers: bait and switch, fake sales, lowballing, and fraudulent representa- ion. Since 1960, a number of major consumer-protection laws have been assed by Congress including The Consumer Bill of Rights, The Food and Drug dministration, Federal Communication Commission, The Postal Inspection iervice, and Better Business Bureau. Many remedies are available to consum- rs who feel they have been fraudulently abused by businesses including self- ielp groups, small claims courts, consumer groups (ACLU), state courts, ederal courts, and class action lawsuits.

Helping students understand their consumer rights and responsibilities is the first step toward becoming a knowledgeable consumer. Internet activities that enhance student understanding of consumer rights and responsibilities are:

- Look for a deceptive practice on the WWW where the Web site promises money and/or prizes if the buyer provides the names of prospects.

- Browse the Internet for a specific period of time to see how many companies require a credit card number before allowing individuals to visit their Web sites.

- Review a recent court decision involving the Internet and determine if consumer rights were violated.

Students and teachers will not be disappointed in the rich libraries of information on the Internet concerning consumer rights and responsibilities. Students can compile and organize a booklet featuring printed (downloaded) documents that highlight one or more of the following: examples of consumer rights; examples of how societal needs are balanced against individual's rights and responsibilities; examples of informative, protective, and enabling consumer laws; examples of greater consumer protection that have resulted in additional costs; examples of local and state consumer organizations, businesses, or government agencies providing consumer assistance; examples of legal alternatives available to consumers for resolving disputes; examples of misleading advertisements; examples of steps that can be taken by victims to gain redress; examples of various types of consumer fraud; and examples of fraudulent, misleading, and legitimate product claims.

Careers

Before money can be spent, it must be earned. Jobs enable individuals to buy the goods and services they need. Work can be very satisfying, bring recognition to the individual, and enable long-range goals to be accomplished. The study of careers may be incorporated into each of the above basic business and personal finance subject areas or grouped together as a major project. By using the Internet, classroom teachers can access and utilize up-to-date information related to possible career choices of students. The Internet increases options available to students for researching their career decisions and obtaining information from the U.S. Occupational Outlook Handbook and other pertinent Web sites.

There are many well-developed sources of career information on the Internet that enable students to:

- Describe careers in which they have an interest and wish to explore.

- Develop their personal career interests, abilities, and goals.

- Explain how consumer demands determine the availability of jobs.

- Identify trends which cause the labor market to change and impact the job market.

- Formulate a career plan that incorporates the entrance requirements of educational and/or training institutions along with tuition costs and student loan availability.

- Determine how geographic location of jobs impact job selection — salary, lifestyle, and cost of living.

- Identify what happens following a job offer. How can the Internet help in the decision-making processes related to relocation costs, housing, schools, and crime statistics?

Career exploration on the Internet is exciting and challenging. The following sample instructional unit (Krewson, 1996) takes approximately five different class periods or one week to complete. The unit is divided into four or five different activities — one activity may be completed each day of the week or they may be distributed over a longer time period.

First, each student is to select a career he or she is interested in exploring. The required level of education or training, the starting salary, and a job description should be determined for each of the chosen careers (U.S. Occupational Handbook is a possible Web site). Next, the current supply and demand for the occupation and the growth projections for the industry should be examined (U.S. Industrial Outlook is a potential Web site). The next step is to research where, geographically, one would have to establish residency in order to get the job (City Net is an applicable Web site). The final step of this careers exploration activity is to have each student decide whether or not to accept a job offer. Students are expected to determine how the cost of living, relocation costs, crime statistics, etc. are related to taking the job.

This careers activity enables students to discover on their own some of the resources available on the WWW. Students are also encouraged to use printed materials and assess the helpfulness of the various sources of information available for making career decisions. The unit can be enhanced by assigning point values to specific career-related items found on the Internet.

Summary

The rich instructional/learning resources made available through Internet, Web sites, and e-mail access have tremendous educational potential. E-mail allows students and teachers to communicate with each other, with companies, and with other individuals and classrooms throughout the world. Basic business and personal finance information on the WWW is vast and continues to increase. Both teachers and students benefit from the use of this medium by being able to explore a multitude of up-to-date content specific resources. These resources allow teachers to expand their classrooms to include the world. Students using the Internet to enhance their learning of basic business and personal finance also gain a basic understanding of electronic communication as well as business applications of the Internet. The Internet skills gained will enable students to achieve success in their future educational course work and professional careers.

References

Krewson, S. (1996, September). *Internet Instructional Activity.* Lesson Plan Developed in Methods of Teaching Business Education Class, University of Missouri-Columbia, Columbia, Missouri.

Weston, C. (1996, September). *Enter the Internet—You Will Not Get GIGO With This Instructional Activity.* Lesson Plan Developed in Methods of Teaching Business Education Class, University of Missouri-Columbia, Columbia, Missouri.

56

Chapter 6 — Internet Tools

by Ken Quamme
University of North Dakota - Williston — Williston, North Dakota
and
Kent Quamme
Fergus Falls Community College — Fergus Falls, Minnesota

When you drive down the highway, you are not really "using" the road in the sense of physically "doing" anything with the road. Instead you are using your car, which happens to work the best on the road. Your car actually uses the road to perform its duty of getting you somewhere. This analogy illustrates that you do not really use the Internet; instead, you use tools that use the Internet (The University of Delaware, 1995).

A clear understanding of the nature of the Internet is important in order to fully appreciate the Internet tools. It is equally important to find tools that are free or inexpensive and easy to use.

As the 20th century winds down, people could ask themselves: "What has brought the world closer together?" Some people, who think about the beginning of the 20th century, would say air travel. Others, referring to the middle of the century, might mention a world war. In the 1990s, when information has become the most prized commodity, people might say "the Internet."

What is "the Internet?" Most people think of the Internet as a thing, an object to use. The Internet is not so much an object as a means for people to get around. Similar to the way people use the current interstate system to travel around the country, cybertravelers use this interconnection of networks called the Internet to make their way around the world.

Is the Internet a passing fad? No! It is here to stay. Since its commercial opening in 1987, the Internet has grown exponentially and has become a household word. In fact, it is such a popular tool of business and the household that there has even been talk of Internet II, a separate Internet restricted to research institutions, universities, and higher education in general. This dual model would lessen the traffic of the original Internet and also allow

Internet II to do what Internet I was originally designed for — educational and scientific research sharing.

The tools addressed in this chapter are Internet tools, not to be confused with desktop, system, multimedia, or applications tools. This chapter is dedicated to the many tools used on the Internet and will help business educators keep up with exploring and finding the right tools to assist Internet users. By knowing about several Internet tools, business educators are more inclined to make effective use of the Internet in their curricula.

58

What Are Internet Tools?

There are many application and software programs that make Internet information available and easy to use. Internet tools are software programs that allow people to use a communications network to its greatest potential. Internet tools are additional utilities that perform or automate various jobs. Internet tools or utilities, that this chapter explores, include the following core set of tools or those most commonly used such as:

- Electronic Mail
- File Transfer Protocol (FTP)
- World Wide Web Browsers
- Search Engines
  - Lycos
  - WebCrawler
  - InfoSeek
  - Yahoo
  - Magellan
  - SearchPal
- World Wide Web Design Tools
  - HTML editors
- Internet Audio and Video Conference
  - Voice Mail
- Internet Filtering
- Point Cast Network
- Utilities/Plug-Ins
  - Knowit All
  - Graphic Viewers/Converters
  - Winzip/Pkware
  - Uuencode/Uudecode
  - Mime Encoder/Decoder
  - Audio/Video Players

Because Internet standards are changing so rapidly, these tools are expected to be periodically upgraded and possibly (and more than likely) will change by the time you read this chapter.

le Transfer Protocol

File Transfer Protocol, better known as FTP, is one of the earliest tools
ed on the Internet. FTP is an efficient way of transferring any type of file.
rly versions of FTP required designation between two file types — binary or
CII. On the one hand, text files were transmitted over the Net in ASCII
rmat; on the other hand, graphics or other types of files usually required the
P software to be set to binary format. These settings were necessary for
ccessful transmissions.

FTP can be used for many things such as downloading software, upload-
g a Web page to a server, and transferring files from one machine to an-
her. Anonymous FTP, as it is commonly called, can be used to download
ftware such as screen savers, application upgrades, and special driver files.
ther software that can be downloaded from the Internet using FTP includes
mmercial demonstration software, shareware, and freeware. Once down-
aded, these packages can be tested and even purchased online. In fact,
ery time a file is downloaded, an FTP is being used.

A Web browser (described later in the chapter) can be used as an FTP,
o. This is, for the lack of a better term, the easiest way to download files.
owever, there are a couple of disadvantages to using a Web browser as FTP
ftware. First, it only allows for downloading files. It does not allow upload-
g a file from one machine to another. Second, only one file can be trans-
rred at a time. Many files in a directory can not be selected for transfer.

FTP was created early on in the development of the Internet when most
ternet users had programmer backgrounds. For this reason FTP has not had
very user-friendly interface. Generally, FTP users must know the exact
ame of the file, the directory in which it is located, and the domain name of
e computer in which the file is stored. FTP is not the "easiest to use"
ternet tool.

lectronic Mail

Electronic mail, e-mail, has been around as long as the Internet and is
ill the most popular tool of the Net. Bill Gates, CEO and founder of Microsoft
orporation, says e-mail is by far the most important Internet tool for him.
his application allows him to keep in touch with his business anywhere he
avels. Andy Grove, CEO of Intel Corporation, confirmed Gates' assessment
f e-mail.

E-mail allows communication of written, non-interactive messages to
nyone in the world, as long as they have an e-mail address. Non-interactive
an advantage because receivers do not need to be logged on to computers
order for messages to be delivered. Therefore, message receivers can read
mail when they want; they do not have to be interrupted when they are
orking on something else.

E-mail is very fast. Most messages will reach their destination within
inutes — even seconds. One classroom example can be demonstrated by

sending a message between two points. Students can time the transmission and calculate when the message is received. Then students can calculate how long it would take to drive in a car between the two points. Interesting findings can be observed.

Although the advantages of e-mail are numerous, remember there are also limitations. One of the major limitations is that e-mail is not as secure as other communications methods. Electronic mail is sent over the Internet, thus being exposed to hackers and crackers — criminal hackers. A simple Trojan horse virus can capture messages on the Internet and allow the perpetrator to read the message. A system administrator can also read messages that are being transmitted. A good rule of thumb is that a person should not send anything via e-mail that the person wouldn't want to be seen publicly.

E-mail is great for sending short, quick, text-based messages; it can also be used to transfer files. Most of the popular e-mail packages have an "attach ment" feature. This allows senders to "tack on" a word processing document a graphic, or program to the message.

World Wide Web Browsers

The fastest growing part of the Internet is the World Wide Web, better known as WWW, or "the Web." The Internet tool that is used to access the Web is known as a browser.

Browsers are software programs that allow users to view information in text, graphics, video, and audio formats. Another name for a browser is an information viewer. The most popular browsers used today include Netscape Microsoft Internet Explorer, and Mosaic. Businesses, educational institutions, and individuals are creating multimedia hypertext material that is stored on Web servers throughout the world. Browsers can be used to browse gopher sites, FTP sites, news groups, and Web sites. With the addition of plug-ins (which will be discussed in the Utilities Tools section), browsers can allow an educator the ability to read hypertext, view hypergraphics, hear audio, view video, and interact with Web sites.

Search Engines

Search engines are software programs designed to index and search through data stored on the Internet. Search engines can be set to search for information on the entire Internet or just for a local search. A local search is a tool that will allow the user to search all available World Wide Web document on a particular server and return pages matching the search criteria.

Search engines help users locate and retrieve information on the Internet. Also, users can access Web pages and search those pages using keywords. The number of search engines is growing rapidly, and not one search engine satisfies every search.

Not all search engines operate the same, and learning about search engines and how they operate is an important Internet skill. Some popular

arch engines are Yahoo, InfoSeek, WebCrawler, Lycos, Magellan, and Alta
sta.

Some helpful "getting started" search engine hints include case sensitiv-
, phrases, required and prohibited terms, wildcards, and proximity search-
g and Boolean.

CASE SENSITIVITY. A search that uses the lowercase term such as
ointcast" will produce findings that are spelled the same but have varying
se structure. In the given example, Pointcast, POINTCAST, and PointCast
ould be among the words listed. However, if a search was entered as
ointCast," the exact spelling and capitalization would be strictly followed.

PHRASES. When searching words in phrases, enclose the words in
uble quotes. "Point Cast Network" will find only words that are the same as
int Cast Network.

REQUIRED AND PROHIBITED TERMS. To form a requirement that one
the words be included in the document, begin the search with a + symbol.
PointCast would be a required search. To prohibit terms from being in-
uded in a document, begin the search with a - symbol. An example of this
ould be: + "Bill Gates" -Road Ahead. In this example, everything about Bill
ates would be located with the exception of his book, *The Road Ahead*.

WILDCARDS. The asterisk is a wildcard character the searcher is
lowed to use at the end of words or phrases to substitute for a combination
 letters.

PROXIMITY SEARCHING AND BOOLEAN. Users can add the terms
ND, OR, NEAR, and NOT when searching. Some examples would be: "Bill
ates" AND "Microsoft", hot OR cold, cars AND automobiles. Although these
xamples apply to most search engines, these techniques are not standard
mong all search engines.

Another tool that allows the searching of the Internet from any Window-
ased software program is SearchPal. It works with almost any of the search
ngines. This software is activated by selecting and highlighting the text in a
ord processing document, an e-mail message, or a database. Once the text
 highlighted, SearchPal will launch a selected browser and start a search
sing an Internet search engine defined in the setup of SearchPal. A listing of
ternet hits will be displayed for the user. If the user is not satisfied with the
sults of the search, a single click will allow the user to activate another
arch engine and continue searching for the highlighted text.

The benefits of using search engines, especially in understanding and
nowing the specific rules for each search engine, will enhance efforts to find
esired information.

Web Design

Creating and maintaining a Web page is a popular activity! Why?
ecause it is so easy to create one. Available Web editors are so easy to use

that a person does not need any special programming talents. Basically, Web page building is simply a point and click programming language. If users want to place a graphic into a home page, they point at the graphic command icon, browse to find an appropriate graphic, click, and the graphic is destined to dazzle the world. This has made Web editors very popular because the simple process allows someone to create a home page and show her or his interests to an entire global community.

Creating a good Web page still requires that the page designer put some work into it. This means knowing the codes for text, tables, frames, and graphics. Also, it means knowing what kind of graphics look best on a page and where to place those graphics. Inasmuch as a Web page developer can "go overboard" on graphics and text, a well-constructed Web page is a product of "old-fashioned" planning.

The World Wide Web displays electronic documents that are written in Hypertext Markup Language or HTML. There is a new type of document being displayed on the Web. It is called Virtual Reality Markup Language or VRML. This expands Web documents by allowing a viewer to "walk through" the page. Web pages are in the truest sense multimedia documents. Editor programs allow page builders to combine text, graphics, audio, and video on one page. Browsers working cooperatively with plug-in programs can turn lifeless screens into multimedia screens with color, sounds, movement, and, last but not least, interaction with the user.

There are several issues influencing the choice of editor programs for building Web pages. One factor that will influence the choice is the platform (Windows, Macintosh, or others) where documents will be created. Hotdog Pro, for example, is available only on a Windows platform. Others, such as Page Mill from Adobe, are available on both Macintosh and Windows operating system platforms.

Some editors can inspect the HTML code and notify the developer if the code is not correct. Additionally, some of the editors will not permit any incorrect code. Some editors provide drag and drop capability to place image on the page. Many Web authoring tools or editors display a view of the page via a Web browser; others let the developer see it in the editor exactly as it wi appear on the Internet.

Most of the companies selling HTML editor programs offer a demonstra tion period to test the product, whereas some companies even promote their editors as freeware or shareware. To find editor programs on the Internet, use one of the many search engines (described in this chapter) or do a search for "web AND editor" or "web AND design."

Internet Audio and Videoconference

The Internet can be used as a telephone and television. These functions can be useful to business and education. For example, a business-person could attend a meeting in one city while being located in one office n another city. A guest speaker could be invited into a classroom at any ime and not have to worry about vehicles breaking down or planes not rriving on time.

Does this mean every business, school, or home needs to have its own elevision studio? Of course not! Does this mean that to see and hear Steinar n Norway we need to spend many dollars on phone bills? Not anymore; we ave the Internet.

Internet audio and videoconference are taking off, and they can be ccomplished for under $300. The authors of this chapter do this all the time. Kent sits in an office in Fergus Falls, Minnesota, and communicates with Ken in Williston, North Dakota. A full-blown televideo conference has been achieved, ncluding color video at 20 frames per second and uninterrupted voice. The quality of the video and sound depends on the volume of Internet traffic. The authors believe this teleconference benchmarked the first cyberfamily reunion n history! Kent's wife Marian, his newborn daughter Alicia, and Kent were ble to visit with Ken and his family, Ken and Kent's sister and her family, and heir mother via Ken and Kent's videophone software. Currently the authors re in the process of setting up cyberlectures for their respective classes.

Audio and visual conference technology will allow many new options in ducation, business, and in home use such as interviewing for jobs, sales neetings, personal meetings, collaborative work between researchers using hared applications, presentations, conference calls, educational classes, game laying, and visiting over coffee with friends and relatives.

Internet Relay Chat has been around for a few years and is still a very opular form of conferencing over the Internet. IRC allows someone to log on o a server (Efnet, Undernet, or Dalnet), go into one of the many channels nline, and chat with people using text. It is a very fast and efficient way of ommunicating but is not very conducive to showing emotion or personalities. On the upside, it does not utilize much bandwidth.

Audio Internet conferencing is very popular and easy to use because all hat is needed is an Internet connection, the software (usually shareware lownloaded from the Internet), a sound card, and a microphone. This allows ommunication with people from all over the world for the mere cost of an nternet connection fee. Internet Phone and Webphone are just two of the udio Internet conference packages available.

There are some limitations to this audio communication. One is that not ll of the software is full duplex. Some software is only half duplex transmis-ion. Full duplex sounds like a telephone — both parties can talk at the same ime. Half duplex sounds like a citizens band radio. When communicators vant to talk, they press a button, and a person on the receiving end must wait ntil the person transmitting the message is finished. This is the polite way. Some small long distance carriers and telephone companies have been trying o curtail the use of Internet audio communication saying it is infringing on heir livelihood.

Usually with audio Internet conference and IRC, users log on to a server. Servers can be programmed to list who is logged on and who is using audio conference software. After knowing who is logged on and what kind of conference software they have, a connection can be established and communication can begin. Some of the software packages can direct connect via the persons' IP (Internet Protocol) address. Direct connect means point-to-point (from one computer to another) without accessing a server to make the connection.

Videoconferencing on the Internet is also becoming popular. People can conduct meetings from the comfort of their own offices. This form of Internet conference allows for voice and video. Also, it can allow electronic and personal presentations as well as file sharing. A student in education could be at home and need help with a spreadsheet problem. The student could call the teacher during cyberoffice hours, meet face-to-face, bring the spreadsheet up on the teacher's screen, and work with the teacher to solve problems.

Generally, video cameras can be purchased with videoconference software. Shareware videoconference software does exist. CuSeeMe is one shareware program that can be found on the Internet. By using a shareware package from the Internet, a user may cross platforms. This means the user does not need the same kind of computer or camera to talk to someone. In other words, a PC user may videoconference with a Macintosh user who has a different brand of camera. This versatility can be a significant factor, unlike software programmed only for one camera.

Point Cast Network

The Point Cast Network (PCN) is a news service provided free via the Internet to computer users functioning on a Local Area Network. PCN provides the user with up-to-date information in categories such as sports, news, weather, Internet, companies, and lifestyles.

PCN allows users to personalize the setup according to their interests. Individual users must select the news articles, weather areas (PCN gives choices of 400 cities where the weather forecast may be obtained), sports, or other categories. The user receives the information based on the individual choices that are made. If there is an interest in the stock market, PCN lets the user enter the ticker symbols. PCN then will give updated prices along with charts showing stock trends. The information is updated approximately every hour as long as the computer is on and has an open network connection. A direct connection works best, and PCN does provide this option for modems in the setup.

In order to retrieve the PCN software, PC users must go to the PCN Web site at http://www.pointcast.com with a Web browser, then download the file to a hard drive. The user next follows the easy installation procedures. PCN operates like a screen saver — activating after a predetermined time interval.

64

he screen saver can be activated manually to display screen flashes about local
nd world news, sports scores, weather, and stock prices (Internet, 1997).

An advantage of the Point Cast Network is time saved. Instead of
rolicking around the Internet, news stories and stock prices flash by on the
omputer screen. PCN uses CNN Interactive for its news articles; these are
pdated hourly. The screen saver is a handy item because it not only shows
elected information but also displays advertisements and other information
lirectly from Netscape Navigator.

Point Cast can be useful in the classroom. By selecting certain news or
tock market services, current updates can be monitored by students on an
ourly basis.

nternet Filtering

As fast as the Internet is growing by users of all ages, there is concern
bout young people traveling the Internet without proper supervision and
uidance. Educators must understand that there are abundant resources
vailable to students, and some materials are not appropriate. It is the
esponsibility of the educator and institution to make sure that students do
ot access undesirable material. By installing filtering software, also called
irewalls, on a computer, educators can prohibit access to Web sites that are
ot appropriate for students.

The benefits of Internet filter tools are that they allow the educator to
ontrol students' navigation while they are on the Internet, control students'
ength of time on the Internet, and control students' access to Web sites.
Most of the Internet filtering software programs allow network administrators
o limit navigation to only appropriate Web sites. Examples of some firewall
oftware are Cyber Patrol, SurfWatch, Net Nanny, Internet Filter, CYBERsitter,
KinderGuard, and Specs for Kids.

tilities/Plug-Ins

Utility Internet tools are used to assist Internet operations or activities.
Jtility tools are referred to as plug-ins.

Plug-ins are software programs that work with Web browsers and allow
he users to benefit greatly from the various media formats that are on the
nternet. A Web browser will not fully recognize types of audio, video, and
ther media formats without the use of plug-ins. The user will be able to
watch or listen to the contents of files while they are downloaded. One of the
oroblems with plug-ins is the high demand of RAM. Plug-ins relate to many
ategories such as 3D Plug-Ins, Audio and Video Plug-Ins, and Business Plug-
ns. An example of one brand name plug-in is NetZip, which allows users to
view the contents of a zip file from within the browser.

FILE COMPRESSION UTILITIES. File compression utilities such as
Pkware and WinZip are designed to compress and decompress files.

Compressed files take less time to transfer over the Internet and also take up less space.

VOICE E-MAIL. Voice E-Mail Player is an Internet utility that allows the sending of voice mail to anyone who has an e-mail address. This new and exciting utility enables users to send voice mail and music to contacts all over the world. In addition, this tool allows users to include pictures and photos. It is an "add-on/plug-in" program for a browser.

UUENCODE/UUDECODE. It is important to use the Internet to send documents, but it can be frustrating without the appropriate tools. Many e-mail programs come with built-in encoders and decoders that assist in the transfer of documents via e-mail. If an e-mail program does not have these capabilities, then the user will have to get Uuencode/Uudecode software. Uuencode converts a binary file into an ASCII format that can be sent using e-mail. Uudecode converts the encoded ASCII file back to binary.

MIME ENCODER/DECODER. MIMEncoders allow the user to send files/documents that are created in a specific application through e-mail and not cause the file to lose readability or formatting. The person receiving the e-mail and file can then decode the file back to the original format.

GRAPHIC VIEWERS/CONVERTERS. Graphic Viewers/Converters allow the user to quickly explore image collections from the Internet and then organize them by renaming, copying, moving, and deleting the files.

VDOLIVE VIDEO PLAYER. The VDOLive Player will allow the playing of videos online without the lengthy downloading time. Various Web sites include real-time video.

ADOBE ACROBAT READER. Many documents on the Web are available in portable document format (PDF). PDF is derived from Adobe's PostScript page description language and was developed for viewing, transmitting, and printing documents. Files in PDF are compressed and have an average file size five times less than that of typical word processor files for the same document (Internet, 1997). In order to view and print the documents, one needs to use a PDF viewing software such as Adobe Acrobat Reader. This software can be downloaded and configured on a desktop computer. Once this software is installed, any document in PDF format can be downloaded and stored on a desktop computer viewed by Adobe Acrobat Reader.

KNOWITALL. KnowItAll is a knowledge management software that allows individuals to better organize information that has been discovered and collected from the Internet. KnowItAll works with only a part of a document instead of the whole document. The section of a document is referred to as a "snippet."

URL-MINDER. The URL-Minder is a free service allowing the user to key in a URL, and, when the keyed Web sites change, e-mail will be sent to notify the user of the change. The URL-Minder system checks the URL periodically;

and if the URL does not match, notification is sent. URL-Minder can keep track of Web sites via HTTP, FTP, or Gopher. It is also possible to have URL-Minder perform regular searches on some search engines and send the user e-mail when the search result changes (Internet, 1996, http://barratry.law.cornell.edu).

One thing that URL-Minder will not do is to keep track of links to the Web site the user is requesting. Each URL must be requested separately in order for the URL-Minder to keep track for the user.

67

Summary

The Internet and particularly the World Wide Web have emerged as legitimate and viable ways to communicate information. The Internet has taken away the requirements of place and time. Internet tools are necessary teaching skills. They are navigation instruments that can help students travel the Internet highways and explore the world's information. Internet tool instruction that teachers provide can assist these global travelers. The instruction makes traveling the Internet easier, more colorful, animated, and exciting. Also, Internet tool instruction provides career skills and online information management.

At a time when Internet access is so critical and competitive for graduating students at all levels, the use of Internet tools is vital for educators and students.

Chapter 7 — The Development of an Internet-Based Course Support System for an Introductory Computer Course

by William C. Ward, III
Kent State University - Trumbull Campus — Warren, Ohio

Computer and communications technologies are changing the way we ve. Higher education is not exempt from this phenomenon. The reality is 1at higher education is charged with leading and preparing both organiza- ons and individuals to adapt to this technological revolution. The demand or computer courses, computerized training, and methods of delivering omputerized instruction are growing at phenomenal rates while educators of ll types struggle to fill these demands. Traditional methods of pedagogy (i.e. ynchronous lectures) simply do not meet the needs of today's students. tudents today want flexibility and learner-based, outcome-oriented educa- ons. They require both synchronous (live classroom) and asynchronous)utside of class) methods of delivery.

Distance education methods are one method of satisfying students' emands. Distance education is playing a greater role in the delivery of ourses, and it will continue to do so. Distance education methods, along with lassroom instruction, meets students' needs for flexibility through asynchro- ious delivery and helps higher education keep pace with the demand for omputer instruction.

The focus of this article is how Kent State University's regional ampuses computerized instruction and distance education computer ourses to meet diverse student needs. An Introduction to Computers ourse at Kent State University was targeted as a starting point to imple- nent this undertaking.

Steven W. Gilbert, director of the American Association of Higher ducation (AAHE) Technology Projects (1995), summarized the impacts of istance learning strategies:

> *Distance Education is any form of teaching and learning in which teacher and learner are not in the same place at the same time, with information technology their likely connector. Of course, faculty members have known for a long time that not every student has to be in the same room all the time with a teacher to learn effectively* (p. 1).

70　 This analogy was the foundation for this project.

Overview of Kent State University

Kent State is a Carnegie Level II institution located in Kent, Ohio. The university offers a broad range of programs and services to individuals and organizations. There are eight physical locations in the Kent system throughout eastern Ohio. The Kent and Stark campuses focus on baccalaureate and graduate programs, while the remaining campuses traditionally focus on two-year associate degree programs and the first two years of baccalaureate programs. In 1996, the regional campuses merged with the School of Technology. Their focus was aimed at technological training programs that included industrial and business training through master's degrees in technology. A new high technology and manufacturing center was approved for completion in 1997 at the Trumbull campus in Warren, Ohio.

Kent State University is also deeply committed to distance and distributed education programs. The university is aligned with IBM Corporation to develop a distributed learning (distance education with computerized instruction) system that is located in the Kent campus library and will be housed in newly renovated Moulton Hall. Each regional campus has at least one distributed education lab (computer-based), one distance learning lab (two-way interactive television), and multiple computer labs with full, no-cost Internet access. By 1997, the regional campuses plan to be connected with Lotus Notes software. The development of distance education courses in all programs was determined to be essential to the success of the university.

Kent State University's Computer Technology Program

The history of the computer technology program at Kent State began in 1970 with the Trumbull campus offering the first associate degree program. The focus was on mainframe computer applications, and by 1985 all of Kent State's regional campuses with the exception of the Stark campus were offering the program. Currently, the program focuses on personal computer operations and applications, networking, and Internet usage. It abandoned mainframe computer applications.

The Trumbull campus currently has the largest number of students enrolled in introductory computer courses and also has the highest number of computer associate degree graduates. The curriculum for computer technology is overseen by a curriculum committee comprised of full-time computer technology faculty members; in addition, each campus is encouraged to have an active advisory board of individuals employed within a local computer industry. According to Dr. Dana Ormerod, associate professor of technology:

Each of the campuses is located in a different geographic and economic area. The computer technology needs of each of these communities differ. Therefore, the task of the faculty is to engender a curriculum which would meet basic academic requirements and at the same time, meet the employment needs of their respective constituent community. Since the establishment of the program in 1970, the faculty and administration have been striving to meet this basic objective (Ormerod, 1995).

71

Course: Introduction to Computers

The introductory course most students take is COMT 11000 (abbreviation for computer technology), Introduction to Computers. A freshman-level course focused on building computer literacy and proficiency, it is the first course taken by novice computer users. It also acts as a service course for several other associate degree programs in business, education, and other technical programs. Many students in baccalaureate programs and others who need basic computer skills take this course. The course is taught by full-time computer technology faculty, but often many adjunct faculty members are needed to teach the course as well. The course is offered at remote sites such as the General Motors Assembly plant in Lordstown, Ohio; Chrysler Plant in Twinsburg, Ohio; and Amitek-Lamb manufacturing in Kent, Ohio.

Purpose of This Project

The primary purpose for instituting this project was to provide Internet Web-based support materials for the Introduction to Computers course. The Internet was chosen as a medium of delivery for several reasons. It is an evolving technology impacting both individuals and institutions, as well as an accepted communications medium among computer users. Also, the Kent State system had Internet access in most computer labs. Another reason the Internet was accepted is because current and comprehensive materials pertaining to computer usage are available on the Internet. The Internet and World Wide Web (WWW) lend themselves to individualized learning. Students can learn at their own pace and follow their own path to information.

This project was designed to be a team approach that involved two technology graduate students and an undergraduate student working on his or her bachelor's degree in technology. The team was supervised by a graduate faculty member from the School of Technology. It received additional support from members of the computer technology curriculum committee. It was viewed as essential to the success of the project that team members were included in the planning and review of the project.

Internet-Based Versus Traditional Instructional Methods

The Internet is a tool that allows students to pursue their educational objectives at their own pace in a Web-like or spherical fashion versus traditional linear or point-to-point methods of instruction. The ability to move forward and backward and to "follow one's own path" to sites can be an effective tool for learning computers or other related subject matter. The greatest benefit of Internet instruction can also be the biggest obstacle to learning. A learner can quickly become lost, lose focus, or drift into unrelated areas. The challenge of utilizing Internet-based instructional materials was recognized during this project.

The Internet can be an effective learning tool and can provide course delivery in a distance education mode. Distance education courses have a tendency to favor disciplined learners and to be extremely difficult for non-disciplined learners. Generally experienced students like distance education courses. Using the Internet as a distance education tool for a freshman level course of new students seemed to contradict the philosophy of a successful distance education project. Therefore, this project was designed to support good instructors with current and innovative technology and technological services to overcome freshmen biases.

One of the major challenges the group faced in designing this project was to allow both learner and instructor flexibility. All Kent State University courses have approved basic data sheets. A requirement for this project was to adapt the methods of delivery to conform to the basic data sheet. The group realized that this project was not foolproof. All attempts were made to construct modules that focused on the broadly defined topic areas within the course, while at the same time allowing for the instructor and the student to remain focused on course content. The nature of the Internet made this problem more challenging than traditional textbook and lecture instructional methods.

Goals Developed for This Project

Goals for this project were developed by team members in conjunction with guidance from the computer technology curriculum committee. The guidelines of basic data sheets were also followed. Establishment of well-defined, measurable goals was critical to the overall success of this project. The following goals were:

- **Goal #1.** Establish a uniform method of course delivery over an eight-campus system.

- **Goal #2.** Establish an introductory computer course that combines computer theory and application.

- **Goal #3.** Design instructional materials that allow the student learner to pursue his or her own path to learning course materials. At the same time, the materials must be designed to allow for continuity of course outcomes for all students.

- **Goal #4.** Enhance the students' overall computer literacy and terminology.

- **Goal #5.** Establish modules of instruction that could be used by all instructors while in the classroom.

- **Goal #6.** Provide instructional materials for students that can be accessed any time, anywhere, and are not dependant upon live classroom instruction.
- **Goal #7.** Develop a methodology for assessing students' successful completion of the course and the skills acquired within the course.

Developing the Project and Making the Team Assignments

Development of the topics or modules is described next. Team members established a listserv for all members of the computer technology curriculum committee. Next, e-mail messages were distributed to all members of the list asking for their input about major topics on the Web page. Their responses were collected from the listserv and categorized. After discussion by the team members, the following topic areas were addressed in the project. Each topic area was developed into a module. A list of the topics/modules follows.

- Introduction (background of the course and program)
- Computer History
- Computer Concepts
- Computer Hardware and Software
- Networks
- Telecommunications
- Internet
- Word Processing
- Spreadsheets
- Emerging Technologies
- Careers in Computers
- PC Webopedia (computer glossary/encyclopedia)

After the curriculum topics were identified, the next step looked at ascertaining system hardware requirements; determining the necessary software; assigning tasks to the team members; using Web-based applications to build modules that directly corresponded to the identified topics; establishing the Web site and home page; and developing JavaScript applications.

HARDWARE REQUIREMENTS. Each team member for this project was required to have access to an IBM compatible computer, a connection to the Internet, scanner, digital camera, and other multimedia applications. All team members had their own computers as well as 24-hour access to the Trumbull campus computer network.

SOFTWARE REQUIREMENTS. Team members could use any Web browser software; however, they selected Netscape 3.0 as the standard because of its availability to faculty and students. Team members had their choice of an HTML editor. They selected Windows Notepad as an HTML editor because it provided good flexibility and allowed the team to design Web page in the desired format.

ASSIGNMENT OF TASKS. The team decided to assign tasks among three members based upon each member's strengths and backgrounds. Darren Gross agreed to develop the JavaScript applications and maintain the technical side of the project. Deb Murphy had a background in telecommunications, networks, and the Internet. She also was responsible for establishing the glossary. Will Ward was responsible for the remaining categories, while Dr. Larry Jones monitored the progress of the group.

BUILDING AND DESIGNING THE MODULES. The first step in this process was to design a uniform look for all the modules. The group agreed upon a common background color, text font and color, object alignment, and logo—the seal of Kent State University. The group chose to use a background and fonts that looked good when viewed with 16-color video drivers that existed on the regional campus network monitors. The home page was a backdrop of a typical syllabus used by the faculty at the Trumbull campus. Trumbull campus faculty, who taught this course, agreed to use standardized textbooks and syllabi. The team members also agreed to limit the use of frames and extensive graphics in order to speed up the downloading process for faculty and students.

The modules, listed earlier, contained Web pages designed by team members and external links to Internet sites. An example of an external link would be a link to Microsoft Corporation (http://www.microsoft.com). This site would be used to view software. Students could then access the actual software manufacturer and obtain information about the product, upgrades, technical support, and costs. The design was such that a faculty member could customize the topics without sacrificing the "common delivery" of the course content. The external links attached to the project's Web page were key components of the overall success of the project. Team members felt that external linking provided the most current course content, as well as served to build students' computer literacy and Internet skills.

The focus of the internally designed pages was to provide the understanding of general computer principles similar to material covered in textbooks and lectures. Terminology and basic computer operations such as hardware and software were covered as well as computer theory and history. URLs and external links were available on the project's home page. This address is found at the end of this chapter.

The modules were designed to meet the overall topic areas that were established from basic data sheets and the computer technology curriculum committee. The group assigned the development of the modules to a team member familiar with that particular topic. The modules were designed so that they could be connected to the site's home page. The modules were designed to be friendly to the user and accessible in an efficient manner. The regional campuses were interconnected and linked.

The regional campus system as a whole has adopted the Microsoft Office Suite as the primary software package for use in the Introduction to Computers course. Microsoft Word, Excel, and PowerPoint were the primary applications covered in this course. The group did provide links to Microsoft and to sites offering information on individual software applications. Microsoft's database program, Access, was not normally covered in this course and was not included.

The university was also affiliated with IBM/Lotus. The Lotus SmartSuite was available at a very minimal cost to Kent State students, staff, and faculty. Many employers at campus sites continued to utilize Corel's WordPerfect. Therefore, the team felt it necessary to link to sites related to both Lotus and Corel. The team did not develop specific in-class, hands-on applications for this project. That was left to the discretion of the faculty member teaching the course.

ESTABLISHING THE WEB SITE AND THE HOME PAGE. The final step to make this project workable was to establish the home page and World Wide Web site. Deb Murphy had both the experience and access to the file server located at Kent State Trumbull campus. She served as the coordinator and created the home page as well as the links to various modules on that site.

Ms. Murphy was responsible for loading all materials onto this site. Team members were able to view documents and test their links. Dr. Jones was able to view the Trumbull site and provide feedback. Team members kept in touch on a regular basis via e-mail, telephone, and face-to-face contact. The team felt that a uniform look at all sites was necessary for the project, including the syllabus background, font color and size, and the appropriate use of graphics.

INCORPORATING JAVASCRIPT APPLICATIONS. JavaScript is a fairly new Internet language. It can be used to bring life, and to some degree, animation to Web pages. The group felt the incorporation of JavaScript examples would be a nice enhancement but not a necessity. Part of the reason for this decision was that not all Web browsers support JavaScript applications. Early versions of Netscape and Microsoft Explorer could not interpret this language.

Analysis of Major Curriculum Topics Connected to the Home Page

Each module (major curricular topic) that is linked to the home page will be discussed.

INTRODUCTION. The home page site provided the basic information about the computer technology program, including the necessary courses for an associate degree. This site also contained information pertaining to a graduate follow-up survey and a brief history about the program. Historical information was authored by Dr. Dana Ormerod. Pertinent information was provided about introductory materials for students majoring in computer technology. This information also served as marketing information.

The following links were incorporated into this module:

- **Link to Computer-Related Sites.** A list of multiple sites all associated with computers and computer usage was available.

- **Metacrawler.** This link could be used to search multiple search engines for specific topics.

- **Netscape Search Engines' Computer Locations.** Excite, Yahoo, Infoseek, Lycos, Magellan.

- **100 Top Web Sites.** This link contained interesting sites encompassing a variety of topics.

The links provided good flexibility for faculty and students to search for information on the Internet. Metacrawler allowed users to search through multiple search engines simultaneously, and this site reflected a massive effort to link many locations directly relating to computer technology. In theory, an instructor could teach the course from this page alone using search engines and existing links to develop lectures.

COMPUTER HISTORY. This section was developed by the team and incorporated various resources pertaining to computer history. It consisted of a brief summary of the five generations of computers and the significant events that occurred within each time period. This section was considered good background information. Other computer history sites were linked to this location and were available for student use.

COMPUTER CONCEPTS. This section was designed as an introduction to computer usage and for hands-on applications used throughout the course. It included basic concepts of computer literacy and workings. It also discussed the four steps of computer processing (input, processing, output, storage), the advantages of using computers, and the disadvantages of using computers.

HARDWARE AND SOFTWARE CONCEPTS. This site was developed by the team to be a good overview of both hardware and software. More extensive information included textbooks, lectures, hands-on applications with various hardware components, and links to various sites on the Internet. The following hardware topics were identified as essential knowledge:

- Computer Start-Up Process
- Central Processing Unit
- BUS Structure
- Motherboard
- Storage Devices
- Key Points About Microprocessors
- Computer Memory and Storage
- Byte Sizes
- Other Types of Memory
- Storage

- Storage Devices
- Hardware Input Devices
- Hardware Output Devices

The following software topics were identified as necessary:

- User Interface

- Major Operating Systems
- Steps Involved for Creating a Program
- Major Programming Languages and Their Primary Users

NETWORKS. Students taking computer courses at the university were working on networks. Many of these students were on a network at their work sites as well. Computer usage is moving away from the concept of each person having an individual machine with his or her own programs toward the concept of one central computer that controls the software applications for multiple machines. Even though networking is closely related to hardware and software usage, the group felt it should be addressed as a separate topic. This module included telecommunications and its affiliation with computers. In general, it was felt students should have knowledge about a network system and how it works. The following topics were covered under networks:

- What Is a Local Area Network?
- How Local Area Networks Work
- Basic Local Area Network Topology

External Links Pertaining to Networks

- Network Basics
- Common Networking Questions
- Basics of Networking
- Networking Basics
- Local Area Networks
- Novell
- Microsoft
- Lantastic

TELECOMMUNICATIONS. The area of telecommunications is closely related to networks. The topics covered in this area were modems, how modems work, modem speeds, and modem uses. The external links were:

- Basic Modem Problems
- Information About Modems
- ITC Home Page
- Newspage

INTERNET. The Internet has become a critical component of Introduction to Computers. Internet use and Internet information were included in this module. Internet topics included:

- History of the Internet
  - What the Internet Is and Is Not
  - Where the Internet Is Headed
- History Links
  - Hobbes' Internet Timeline
  - Introduction to the Internet — History
  - Internet History Lessons and Links
  - *How the Internet Came to Be* by Vinton Cerf
  - How Did We Get Here Anyway?
  - Internet History v. 1.0.1
  - When Did the Internet Start?
  - A History of Computers and the Internet
  - RFC1206 — Answers to Commonly Asked "New Internet User" Questions
  - As We May Think
  - A Little History of the World Wide Web
  - A Not Terribly Brief History of the Electronic Frontier Foundation
- Other Links Related to the Internet
  - Where Is the Digital Highway Really Headed?
  - Is There a Place for the Have-Nots in Cyberspace?
  - Internet Freedom and Our Children's Future
  - The Information Future Out of Control
  - Growing Our Communications Future

WORD PROCESSING APPLICATIONS AND TERMINOLOGY. Word processing was one of two primary hands-on applications covered in the course. Spreadsheets was the other. The group felt that students needed the theoretical background, as well as the appropriate terminology associated with word processing applications. They felt strongly that students needed to know why to push buttons, not just how to push them. Topics covered in this section included word processing principles, word wrap, portrait versus landscape printing, types of fonts, line spacing, and additional word processing features.

SPREADSHEETS. This section followed the same logic as word processing applications. Spreadsheet applications are the second major type of software application taught in this course. This module provided general background information on spreadsheet usage. The following external links were incorporated.

- Spreadsheet Basics
- Introduction to Math and Spreadsheets
- Lotus 1-2-3: The Basics
- Excel Basics
- Quattro Pro Basics

EMERGING TECHNOLOGIES. This section was a series of links to "current" technologies that are emerging. It is by no means an exhaustive list and to some degree was outdated the day it was created. This page gave faculty members a way to show students some related technologies that could affect them as computer users. The areas identified were artificial intelligence, client-server applications, virtual reality, Web browsers, telecommunications, cable modems, and distance learning with computers.

CAREERS IN COMPUTERS. This page was dedicated to career-related sites. Many students taking Introduction to Computers were unsure of their future and had not declared their major. The group felt that it was imperative to assist students with career exploration or selection of a major program of study. The goal was not to convert all students to computer technology majors, but to show students how computers and the Internet could become essential parts of a career. The external links to this site were:

- Job Seeker's Workshop . . . Choosing a Career — Here's Looking at You!
- Getting a Job With Computers
- Using Library Resources for Career Searches
- Ohio Bureau of Employment Services
- "Monster" Career Service

Summary

This project was a substantial undertaking by a team of computer faculty and support personnel. It was a comprehensive Web document that could be used by both faculty and students in either a synchronous (live classroom) or asynchronous (non-class time period) mode. The project was designed to provide Internet-based instructional modules for the course, Introduction to Computers, with the emphasis on creating a uniform curriculum across all eight-campus locations, while at the same time allowing instructor flexibility and academic freedom. The Web pages were a combination of topics generated by group members and applicable external links to external Web sites.

The use of Internet Web-based instructional materials allowed the instructors and students to maximize access to current materials in a rapidly changing technological environment. Also, it permitted instructors and students to access materials at times that were convenient for them. The course still required an instructor-driven lecture enhanced with hands-on applications of software. Students were able to learn about computer literacy and develop computer-related competencies from this course.

This project was successfully completed due to the group process and interaction among the team members. Each team member was able to use his or her skills and expertise, yet coordinate his or her weaknesses with other team members. The project's success was the result of all the team members knowing each other, cooperative work ethics, and regular communications through face-to-face interaction and e-mail.

Follow-up procedures are in place to improve this project. Evaluations were distributed to faculty who taught the course, and it is expected that feedback, changes, and revisions will be received and enacted. The project was introduced on a trial basis in the classroom during the spring semester (1997).

This project developed supporting material for a course in Introduction to Computers. It did not include the entire course. Its intention was to provide instructional support and materials and not to replace instructors and live classroom experiences.

Because this project was a pilot program, more evaluation needs to be conducted to evaluate its effectiveness as a teaching tool. Due to rapid changes in technology and the Internet, this course required constant updating of materials and associated links. Even though revisions were necessary, materials were generally more current than textbooks and other materials.

Other courses in the computer technology curriculum could use this type of support or have it developed. Upper division and graduate courses seem to be natural fits.

The developing team members are open to any suggestions within and from outside of Kent State University. This project was an experiment and will need iterations of changes. Note: This project is located at http://www.tech.kent.edu/sot/ldj/; click on Introduction to Computers at the bottom of the page, and the outline of this project will appear. Follow the appropriate links.

References

Barton, S., and Ormerod, D. (1995). *Follow-Up Study of Computer Technology Graduates and Their Employers, 1987-1991.* Kent, Ohio: Kent State University Regional Campuses.

Gilbert, S.W. (1995). *Why Distance Education?* AAHE (American Association of Higher Education) Bulletin 3.

Chapter 8 — Online International Business

81

by Robert J. Matyska, Jr.
University of South Carolina — Columbia, South Carolina

The globalization of business has created new patterns, policies, and procedures for collaborating in commercial activities. Within this environment, every one of us fulfills three roles: consumer, producer, and citizen Dlabay and Scott, 1996). As consumers, we make decisions and purchase goods and services; as employees, we work for firms that participate in international trade or compete against those that do; and as citizens, we are represented by our nation in the global arena.

Classroom business educators contribute to the development of secondary and postsecondary students in areas for and about business, as well as foster opportunities to gain leadership skills, all with an eye to meeting the challenges of an increasingly interdependent and technological world. These challenges converge on the Internet, where the professional educator and learners have access to a host of resources for developing invigorating and engaging classroom activities. But taming the vast array of resources and turning them into classroom learning situations can be a daunting task, particularly in the relatively new curricular area of international business.

Teaching and the Internet

The Internet allows teachers and students to access the world beyond their classroom walls, share information, and engage in thought-provoking discussion. The benefits of using the Internet as an educational tool include the wealth of current information available, the opportunity to develop analytical and inquiry-based thinking skills, and the use of active learning strategies (Matyska and Zeliff, 1996). Effectively, the Internet is just a huge computer network; a network of networks in fact. If, as some insist, the

Internet is as much about people as it is about computers, then it is also the global community of over 50 million individuals that have access to it (and that number is growing at a phenomenal rate). Several thousand members of this community are educators from around the globe who are just like you — trying to figure out how to use the vast amounts of information and resources available online to enrich student learning and increase content understanding.

The Internet has been described as a huge library, with plenty of people to talk to and lots of information, essentially free of charge. However, you get what you pay for, as this library has a poor card catalog and effectively no directory of services (Steen, Roddy, Sheffield, and Stout, 1995). So what can you do with this huge mess of wire, telephone cable, binary code, data warehouses, and application software? Harris (1994) recommends developing Internet projects in the following three general areas:

- Interpersonal exchanges — keypals, global classroom exchanges, and electronic mentoring.

- Information collections — information exchanges, tele-field trips, and electronic publishing.

- Collaborative problem solving — information searches, social action projects, and simulations.

The majority of the content on the Internet is information and opinion, but it is up to us, as classroom educators, to devise specific learning activities that leverage these resources. We must discover sites and figure out how to include them in classroom lesson planning. One great idea for developing your own Internet-based international business activities of these types is the WebQuest.

A WebQuest is "an inquiry-oriented activity in which some or all of the information that students interact with comes from resources on the Internet" (Dodge, 1997). This innovative instructional activity developed by Dr. Bernie Dodge, professor of educational technology at San Diego State University, is an excellent way to bring the Internet into your curriculum. Dodge's WebQuests are organized into two levels, short-term and longer term. The short-term projects, designed to be completed in one to three class periods, focus on knowledge acquisition and integration, where learners make sense out of a considerable amount of new information. A longer term WebQuest may last from one week upwards of a month, and focuses on extending and refining a body of knowledge and transforming it in some manner through creation of something new (Dodge, 1997).

While both require a good deal of preparation on the part of the classroom educator, student learning online is greatly enhanced. Most teachers who are familiar with the Internet will agree that there is little educational benefit in having learners wander cyberspace without a task at hand. By following Dodge's guidelines for creating a WebQuest, business educators can be confident that students have guidelines designed to make the best use of their online time.

Guidelines for Creating Good WebQuests

As with any classroom activity, the key to a successful Internet-based experience is planning: planning activities, planning locations, planning how to discriminate between good and bad sites, and planning how to use all this information and organize lessons for student success. Also important is figuring out when using Internet resources makes more sense than using traditional materials such as traditional reference sources and subject-matter experts. According to Dodge (1997), good WebQuest construction focuses on these suggestions and includes the following sections:

- An introduction that sets the stage and provides some background information;

- A task that is accomplishable and interesting;

- A set of information sources needed to complete the task, usually in the form of Internet addresses embedded in the WebQuest document;

- A description of the process learners should go through in accomplishing the task, in clearly described steps;

- Some guidance on how to organize the information acquired, such as timelines, and concept maps; and

- A conclusion that brings closure to the quest, reminds learners what they've learned, and perhaps encourages them to extend the experience into other domains.

Other suggestions include using collaborative learning groups, incorporating cross-disciplinary themes to include other instructors and/or classes, and augmenting the experience through realistic scenarios or role-playing situations where learners step into the content under consideration. Now that you are familiar with the "what" of WebQuests, it is time to get started on the "how" of the process.

As with any curriculum design, start with what you know, or what you are familiar with. Figure out what is available for the business education classroom in general, or how you can tie into other disciplines and content areas. Good starting places for the classroom teacher are:

- Teacher Catalog of Resources

    http://edweb.sdsu.edu/edweb_folder/index/Teacher_Catalog.html

- Web Resources for Educators

    http://edweb.sdsu.edu/edfirst/courses/web_for_ed.html

- Kathy Schrock's Guide

    http://www.capecod.net/schrockguide

Each of these sites includes links to many different subject areas, as well as further investigations on the topic of WebQuests. Once you have wandered the Web for awhile, start to organize your "surfing" by topic and Uniform Resource Locator (URL), and make a few notes about each site you visit relative to content, usefulness, and teaching area. Then brainstorm about the kinds of tasks you could give your students based on what you found and what you are teaching. Next, take a lesson from your current unit or semester plan and start investigating where Internet resources for that plan are located. Categorize the pages and URLs you are accessing by some of the following suggestions: reference materials, subject-matter expert contacts, lesson plans and ideas, searchable databases, class projects, biographies, and instructional tools. Look for areas of your existing lesson plan that can be enhanced or expanded through the use of online materials and information. You now have the foundation for your own WebQuest.

Move into the construction phase with the online WebQuest template at http://edweb.sdsu.edu/sebqquest/TeacherLessonTemplate.html and view examples, save them to your computer, and possibly use them in your own classroom. It is a good idea to consider how you will evaluate student learning as you construct your online project. A great way to assess the final product of a student's or learner group's WebQuest experience is to use alternative assessment tools such as rubrics and checklists. Begin with the end in mind, and you will have a good idea of how to get there as you scour the Internet for resources.

For more information about Dr. Dodge, his WebQuest process, or to view actual examples of excellent WebQuests, visit "The WebQuest Page" at http://edweb.sdsu.edu/webquest/webquest.html, where you will find a host of resources for creating your own Internet-based classroom activities. On the main page, you will find a concept paper on WebQuests, links to Internet sites to get you started, a matrix of projects and content areas to stimulate creativity, and more. There is even a WebQuest about developing great WebQuests at http://edweb.sdsu.edu/webquest/webquestwebquest.html that will take you on a trip through the Internet and have you evaluate other online projects. Dr. Dodge even uses collaborative learning in his WebQuest creation activity. The following sections offer some ideas on Internet activities and content for a course in international business.

International Business Goes Internet

The global nature of the Internet makes it a perfect resource for teaching international business at all levels of education. It is estimated that people from over 120 countries around the world now have Internet access (Steen, Roddy, Sheffield, and Stout, 1995). The challenge of teaching with the Internet is locating appropriate resources and sites that correlate with instructional topics discussed in class. A good place to start is to identify individual instructional goals. Do you want to simply assemble resources for learners to use (similar to turning students loose in a library) or do you want to target some more specific learning outcomes? Both are valid approaches, but both require different strategies for Internet resource identification and collection.

The majority of the following ideas relate to the International Business Standards that are part of the *National Standards for Business Education*

ublished by the National Business Education Association (NBEA, 1995). They
re suggestions for appropriate resources to complement texts and other
naterials used by the classroom educator to cover competencies in an interna-
onal business course or a unit in another course that focuses on international
usiness. These URLs are by no means the only resources available to teach
nese standards and are provided as a starting point for the activity or develop-
ng a more lengthy project, such as the WebQuests outlined above.

85

ANALYZE EXAMPLES OF INTERNATIONAL TRADE. This project
nvolves researching and gathering information about the export/import
ndustry, how the balance of trade impacts a nation's economy, as well as
valuating the benefits of exporting and importing. Starting with the following
esources for exporting and importing, learners can gather information about
vhat is traded and by whom, including how trade impacts economies.

- Export-Import Bank of the United States

    http://www.exim.gov/

- U.S. Export Directory

    http://maingate.net/us-exports/bge.html

Additional investigation into emerging trade powers and what they are
rading and receiving in return can provide a more current or personalized
tudy. As a means of demonstrating mastery of the content, students could
roduce an oral or written report of their research, focusing on a specific
ountry, geographic region, industry, or product line.

**AWARENESS OF MAJOR GEOGRAPHICAL FEATURES AND CITIES OF
HE WORLD.** This activity can be accomplished either in groups or individu-
lly. Students can research and investigate a specific country or economic
rade zone to gain an understanding of other regions of the globe, different
rade zones, and non-western cultures. The country or zone could be as-
igned by the instructor to guarantee adequate coverage and lack of duplica-
ion in research projects or allow learners or groups to select a country of
nterest to them. Students begin researching the following resources for an
stounding variety of statistics on countries, as well as sightseeing, transporta-
ion, and where to stay and dine in major cities around the globe.

- CityNet Travel Essentials

    http://www.city.net/features/essentials

- CIA World Fact Book

    http://www.odci.gov/cia/publications/nsolo/wfb-all.htm

The Fact Sheet at CityNet on each major city covers much of what a
raveler would need to know — customs, language, climate, passport needs,
oltage requirements for personal appliances, holidays, and more. The
ountry page from the World Fact Book covers all aspects of the country —
overnment and economy, people, terrain, transportation, and more. Evalu-
te a written report or have students submit an executive summary of their
eport, which is then presented orally to the entire class. For a fun bit of

closure, groups could provide a sample of local cuisine with a recipe from a very comprehensive database with a wide variety of recipes from the United States and around the world:

- Recipe Database

  ftp://ftp.neosoft.com/pub/rec.food.recipes/

CAREER OPPORTUNITIES. It is never too early to start students thinking about the world of work and how work will be impacted by the world. Using the following online resources, students can research career clusters through the Occupational Outlook Handbook, create and refine a personal job search strategy using First Steps in the Hunt, and access links to schools, position descriptions, and general industry information through the Catapult at the Job Web site.

- Occupational Outlook Handbook

  http://stats.bls.gov/ocohome.htm

- First Steps in the Hunt

  http://www.interbiznet.com/hunt/

- The Catapult

  http://www.jobweb.org/catapult/catapult.htm

A possible end result may be a personal career path portfolio with a detailed analysis of a chosen career or industry, plans for further education to reach these goals, and identification of at least three prospective careers or openings currently listed on the Web. A resume and cover letter targeting one of the vacancy notices are also possible results. Rubrics would be a great evaluation tool for such a final product.

INTERNATIONAL BUSINESS COMMUNICATIONS. An understanding of basic words and phrases in languages other than English is not enough for success when conducting business with partners from outside the United States. Nonverbal issues such as cultural differences, celebrations, and holidays, as well as sports, economic, and other events are essential to interpersonal communications. The following resources can enlighten learners to societies and festivals outside their own culture — both at home and overseas:

- One-World Global Calendar

  http://www.zapcom.net/phoenix.arabeth/1world.html

- World Events Calendar

  http://w3.eventseeker.com/

- Worldwide Holidays and Festivals

  http://www.smiley.cy.net/bdecie/

- Foreign Languages for Travelers

  http://www.travlang.com/languages

Many people involved in international business have traveled overseas, only to discover that there is a national or religious observance going on at the

me time. Proper planning would facilitate appropriate timing for conduct-
g business travel. Also, a basic understanding of the local language (basic
ords, directions, shopping/dining, and times/dates) is essential for travel
utside one's own home country. By clicking on the flag of another country at
e Foreign Languages for Travelers site, students reach a page that provides
th audio (spoken) and written (translating dictionary) resources for travel-
s. Spoken words and phrases allow anyone with a sound card and speakers
hear samples and increase his or her oral language fluency. A variety of
tivities may be designed here, but a basic project involving an investigation
the culture and language of another country could be tied together with
udy in a foreign language classroom or used on its own as a supplement to
e international business classroom.

CURRENCY AND EXCHANGE. International finance, particularly the role
d importance of currency transactions, can be a very interesting part of the
ternational business classroom. Fluctuations in domestic currency, as well as
ose of other countries, are the foundation for a variety of discussions. Included
this area are topics such as the cost of travel overseas, gains and losses in
penses and income due to changes in the value of currency, potential problems
dealing in foreign currencies, and how economic and political conditions at
me and overseas affect currency values. The following exchange rate sites
lculate simple and advanced (multiple) currency exchange transactions, as well
explain how currency exchange rates impact companies:

- Currency Converter

    http://www.oanda.com/cgi-bin/ncc

- Currency Exchange Rates

    http://www.travlang.com/money

Have learners include in their discussion any potential problems of
aling in foreign currencies, as well as a brief discussion of balance of
yments. Present findings orally, and support the discussion with several
readsheet analyses of currency transactions and trackings over at least a
o-week period. Additionally, a spreadsheet graphing exercise tracking the
rrency rates could bring together concepts and applications from several
urses.

TRADE BARRIERS AND AGREEMENTS. In order to understand the
pact of current and emerging trade issues on the United States, the interna-
nal business community, and/or a specific region of the globe, have stu-
nts describe several international trade agreements similar to those found
the following locations:

- GATT Defined

    http://www.econ.iastate.edu/classes/econ355/choi/gatt.htm

- NAFTANet

    http://www.nafta.net/welcome.htm

This activity includes defining why trade barriers are imposed by governments, outlining why agreements are necessary, and assessing the impact of current and emerging trade issues on a specific region. Great as an individual research project or in groups of three or four, this type of activity lends itself well to collaboration with colleagues who teach social studies or government.

ETHICS. Ethical business behavior has taken on a new importance in the classroom, and the Foreign Corrupt Practices Act (FCPA) blends both ethics and international business. After a thorough review of the following sites, a class discussion on business actions that may positively or negatively impact societies and cultures can be initiated.

- FCPA Resource Pages

    http://www.tht.com/ClientBulletinForeignCorruptPracticesAct.htm

    http://juggler.lmsc.lockheed.com/star/950210star/stories/05a foreign.html

The components of the FCPA, particularly the Act's impact on a company's activities at home and on international soil, can lead to very stimulating discussions that broaden a learner's understanding of the way business operates beyond our borders.

PLAN A TRIP OVERSEAS. From a list provided or using an assigned location, have students plan a trip to another country using some of these resources:

- Travelocity Online Reservations

    http://www.travelocity.com
- Worldwide Hotel Database

    http://www.travlang.com/hotels
- Online Tourist Information

    http://garcia.efn.org/ ~ rick/tour/
- International Traffic Signs and Road Rules

    http://www.travlang.com/signs
- Intellicast's World Weather

    http://www.intellicast.com/weather/intl/
- Mastercard's ATM Locator

    http://www.mastercard.com/atm/
- Subway Routes by International City

    http://metro.jussieu.fr:10001/bin/cities/english
- World Electric Guide

    http://www.cris.com/ ~ Kropla/electric.htm
- U.S. State Department Travel Warnings

    http://travel.state.gov/travel_warnings.html

- Foreign Entry Requirements for U.S. Citizens

  http://travel.state.gov/foreignentryreqs.html

The trip can include sight-seeing, cultural events, business tours, or whatever the "traveler" wants to investigate. A great way to present this type of information is to have the learners use desktop publishing software to create an enticing informational brochure or flyer for a fictional travel agency that incorporates several of the above points. These then may be displayed in the classroom bulletin board and even shared with the foreign language department as an enhancement to their studies in that area.

ENTREPRENEURIAL OPPORTUNITIES. This project involves students in the conduct of research and preparation of a short paper about how a U.S.-based business entered the global marketplace in another country. Examples include how Coca-Cola entered China or how Pepsi introduced its product in then-communist countries like the former Soviet Republic; the challenges faced by UPS in entering the European market; or how a company like McDonald's, whose product line is anchored by beef items, opened locations in India. A combination of Internet and traditional resources might be used to complete this activity. An alternative is to split the class in half and have one half use only electronic sources and the other half use only traditional resources. A discussion of the quantity, quality, and recent nature of the information found should prove interesting when the two groups get back together again.

OTHER IDEAS. Have students participate in a WebQuest Project, "Searching for China," to gain an understanding of a distant land by employing resources found at the following site:

- China WebQuest

  http://www.kn.pacbell.com/wired/China/ChinaQuest.html

The site can also be used as an example of a detailed WebQuest to spur your own imagination.

To instill some entrepreneurial skills in your students, why not have groups of learners brainstorm on a product to develop and market globally via the Internet through a Web page storefront presence? Follow these links for tutorials on Hypertext Markup Language (HTML) and clip art, and learn to create Web pages that focus on a product or service:

- HTML Crash Course

  http://edweb.gsn.org/htmlintro.html

- How to Write HTML

  http://www.ncsa.uiuc.edu/General/Internet/WWW/

- Barry's Clip Art Server

  http://www.barrysclipart.com/

Finding Your Own Resources

The preceding activities are only a few of the many ideas that lend themselves to augmenting the international business teacher's classroom activities and materials. Locating Internet sites for activities you design yourself should not be a daunting task. These search engines and tools should prove useful in your investigations:

- Business Researcher's Interests

     http://www.brint.com/interest.html

- All Business Network

     http://www.all-biz.com/

- AltaVista

     http://altavista.digital.com

- Yahoo

     http://www.yahoo.com

- Internet Services List

     http://www.spectracom.com/islist

- HotBot

     http://www.hotbot.com

- The Argus Clearinghouse

     http://www.clearinghouse.net/

- Finding Internet Information

     http://www.bus.orst.edu/tools/other/general/strategy.htm

The Internet Services List is an "A to Z" list covering all types of subjects and a wide variety of Internet tools, from Web pages to TELNET addresses to FTP host machines and more.

It may be helpful to explore the work of your educator colleagues at the following sites:

- Collaborative Plan Archive

     http://faldo.atmos.uiuc.edu/TUA_Home.html

- AskERIC Lesson Plans

     http://ericir.syr.edu/Virtual/Lessons/

- K-12 Lesson Plans

     http://teams.lacoe.edu/documentation/places/lessons.html

- Armadillo K-12 Resources

     http://riceinfo.rice.edu/armadillo/Rice/Resources/databases.html

- Teachers.Net Lesson Plans

     http://www.teachers.net/lessons/

- Teacher Resources

  http://juliet.stfx.ca/people/stu/x94emj/teacher.htm

On these sites, you can see the types of lesson plans designed by teachers around the globe and from almost every academic area, as well as resources for using the Internet in your classroom. Be creative, borrow good ideas from others, and share your successful materials with other educators, through traditional as well as electronic forums.

91

ome Final Tips

The Internet brings new perspectives on teaching and learning and requires educators to adapt present teaching skills to this relatively new electronic instructional medium. Some suggestions include providing specific and concrete instructions for learners, starting the project offline to organize thoughts and strategies, and checking for comprehension by moving from student to student or group to group frequently. The value of the Internet and international business instruction depends greatly upon the kinds of skills and content employed in the classroom by both learners and leaders. Eager minds focused with strong activities, a curiosity for learning, and a certain amount of skepticism regarding the authority of Internet documents will find visits to the Internet incredibly rewarding and informative. Empower your students for a lifetime of success with international business competence and Internet skills—a powerful combination in any career path.

eferences

labay, L. R., and Scott, J. C. (1996). *Business in a Global Economy*. Cincinnati: South-Western Educational Publishing.

odge, B. (1997, May 5). The WebQuest Page. [Online]. Available: http://edweb.sdsu.edu/courses/edtec596/about_webquests.html.

arris, J. (1994, Premier Issue). Types of K-12 Projects on the Internet. *Classroom Connect*, 4.

latyska, R. J., and Zeliff, N. D. (1996). Opening Minds to the Power of the Internet, Part 1. *Instructional Strategies: An Applied Research Series*. Little Rock, AR: Delta Pi Epsilon.

ational Business Education Association. (1995). *National Standards for Business Education: What America's Students Should Know and Be Able to Do in Business*. Reston, VA: National Business Education Association.

teen, D. R., Roddy, M. R., Sheffield, D., and Stout, M. B. (1995). *Teaching With the Internet: Putting Teachers Before Technology*. Bellevue, WA: Resolution Business Press, Inc.

Chapter 9 — Use of the Internet in Management and Marketing

by Bobbye J. Davis
Southeastern Louisiana University — Hammond, Louisiana
and
Josie V. Walker
Southeastern Louisiana University — Hammond, Louisiana

In their continuing struggle to remain competitive in a rapidly changing marketplace, businesses face a variety of challenges and opportunities. Globalization, real-time communication, and efficient resource use are only a few of the challenges businesses encounter. The opportunities afforded by these challenges increase the potential to broaden the marketplace, to supply current information and feedback from customers, and to save time and money. To assist in meeting these challenges and opportunities, today's businesses can utilize the marketing power of the Internet.

The Internet is an excellent vehicle for taking advantage of these challenges and opportunities. However, tapping the resources of the Internet requires an inquiring and adventurous mind, a "can do" attitude, and an innovative spirit. Without these qualities, the novice Internet user could view the Internet as a maze of unrelated, hard-to-locate facts, figures, ideas, and relationships. With these qualities, the innovative businessperson could view the Internet as a gold mine of information and ideas.

Businesses have recognized the demand for "better, faster, and cheaper" products and services and realize that increased employee productivity is one of the means to that end. The technological advantages offered by the Internet respond to this demand, especially in the fields of management and marketing.

Managerial and marketing strategies should include establishing a presence on the Internet's World Wide Web (WWW). This presence will allow responses to marketing and management issues arising in electronic space and provide opportunities for increasing markets, improving customer relations, and providing information for decision-making.

Corporate Use of the Internet

Corporate America is so intrigued with the potential of the Information Superhighway that more and more businesses are unleashing its technological fury and accessing the Internet daily. Businesses are rethinking their whole infrastructure in order to fully integrate telecommunications and computer technology.

94

Expanding development and use of information technology seem to impact the business world more than any other variable today. As shown in a Conference Board Report survey (1995) of executives on information management and communications councils in the U.S. and Europe, 82 percent of the respondents reported having access to the Internet. Of the 18 percent not yet connected, almost all were planning to access the Internet in the near future.

Furthermore, this survey has shown that companies connect to the Internet for several reasons including communication, research, file transfer, and marketing activities.

Internet communication has greatly enhanced the global aspect of business interaction and changed the perspective of marketing and management strategies.

Managerial Strategies

Managers face several challenges as they approach the 21st century. Of these challenges, two major tasks include: (1) promoting businesses on the Internet, and (2) dealing with new aspects of communicating. Pursuing these tasks is complicated by the dynamic nature of the Internet, a situation that requires businesses to be constantly vigilant.

PROMOTING BUSINESSES ON THE INTERNET. Business organizations are rapidly establishing their presence on the Internet by constructing home pages. The Internet medium has grown so fast and has become so influential that this presence is almost mandatory.

Effective home pages attract potential customers and provide essential information to them. Home pages are current, interactive, and informative. When customers access home pages, they expect the most recent information and the ability to link to other resources. They also expect to be able to purchase a product or service, request information, and make comments and/or suggestions. Examples of information included on home pages are:

- Company information (location, company officials, subsidiaries, etc.)
- Products and services (information and purchasing)
- Shareholder information
- Community involvement
- Employment opportunities
- What's new
- International sites

- Search and help options
- Environmental issues

Customer interaction with the home page is measured by the number of times a customer accesses the home page. Counters are generally incorporated in the design of the home page, yielding the number of "hits" (each time a person accesses the home page). Documentation of the number of "hits" and customer feedback are vital information to strategic management planning.

95

Some experts recommend that home pages are more effective when they contain a series of pages instead of including all information on one long, continuous page. Internet "surfers" seem to prefer clicking from page to page as a means of obtaining information rather than scrolling to access information on one long page. In addition, changing the appearance of the home page periodically (about every two months) increases and maintains interest and, thus, results in more people accessing the home page.

Constructing and maintaining a home page provides a viable way of promoting a business and entering the digital revolution (or Webolution) made possible by an Internet whose rapid expansion is changing the way business is being done.

COMMUNICATING. A number of communication tools have been employed by the business world in recent decades. In the 1970s, the three most common methods of communication were in person, by telephone, or by U. S. mail. In the 1980s, fax machines, computers, cellular phones, and e-mail emerged. Today the Internet is the fastest growing communication medium of all time and constitutes the greatest revolution in telecommunications. In fact, some say the Internet could be considered the fourth medium, positioned along with print, radio, and television (Leshin, 1997).

E-mail is the most widely used service on the Internet. Whether dealing with internal or external communication, managers often choose e-mail as the method for correspondence. One of the most valid reasons for using this service is that it saves both time and money.

E-mail provides an easy, convenient, cost-effective way of communicating with suppliers, peers, and customers. This service can replace significant numbers of voice calls, faxes, postal mailings, and face-to-face meetings, thus enhancing work flow. Receivers of e-mail can choose a convenient time to read and respond to messages, thereby increasing productivity.

Because e-mail seems less formal than typical business correspondence, managers and other e-mail users tend to view it as conversation. Actually, e-mail is writing, and bad writing has no place in the e-mail world. E-mail messages should be kept short, and messages are more easily grasped when a subject line is included. Each e-mail message should be limited to one subject; sending separate e-mail messages is better than covering several topics in one message.

Since time savings, cost savings, and facility of use are obvious advantages to e-mail as a communication tool, managers are expected to become proficient in its use and to manage the resultant overload of information. Additionally, geography, time zones, and location will be less limiting since communication can be sent at any time from anywhere across national boundaries.

MANAGEMENT-RELATED WEB SITES. Listed below are examples of management-related Web sites.

- EINet Galaxy's Business and Commerce Directory

    http://galaxy.einet.net/galaxy/Business-and-Commerce.html

- 100 Biggest American Corporations

    http://fox.nstn.ca

- Net2Business — Links to Business Resources

    http://www.commerce.com/net2/business/business.html

- Interesting Business Sites

    http://www.owi.com/netvalue/vlilll.html

- Hot Business Sites

    http://www.hbs.harvard.edu/applegate/hot_business

- CommerceNet

    http://www.commerce.net

Marketing Strategies

The Internet has dramatically changed the direction of marketing. Marketers now have a vehicle that brings them together with customers simultaneously in an interactive, individual fashion. The innovative marketer can take advantage of this opportunity by utilizing the Internet to communicate and gather information about customers and competitors.

COMMUNICATING. From a marketer's perspective, communication is closely related to customer relations. The Internet allows marketers to pay attention to details with more ease and less expense than ever before. Information from communicating on the Internet can be obtained in several ways: one-on-one messaging, listservs, and UseNet groups.

One-on-one messaging or e-mail is direct contact with customers. Access to e-mail is an essential marketing communication tool. Customers can contact companies through e-mail by accessing home pages. Companies gather information from the specific questions or comments made by customers.

Listservs and UseNet, or discussion groups, are used by people who share similar interests. Companies participate in and benefit from these discussion groups by browsing messages and posting responses when appropriate. Since many of a company's customers have access, the Internet becomes a targeted medium for communicating with this audience. For example, a company producing computer equipment can follow a discussion group to see how customers are reacting to the purchase and use of its equipment. Listserv discussions reveal questions asked, complaints made, or simply topics discussed.

A one-on-one relationship with customers is developed by addressing their specific needs, leading to a customer-centered approach to marketing rather than the traditional product-centered approach. The interactivity resulting from use of the Internet through e-mail and discussion groups enhances this transition.

97

GATHERING INFORMATION. Businesses need to conduct market research for a number of reasons: to monitor their competitors' activities, to update themselves on industry events, to analyze new business opportunities, and to find strategic alliance partners in other countries. The Internet is a powerful tool for gathering this and other information for marketers. Both primary and secondary research are successfully conducted on the Internet.

While traditional methods of market research are both costly and time-consuming, conducting primary research on the Internet permits businesses to reach their customers directly and inexpensively. Given the limitations associated with today's average product life cycle of six months, collecting market intelligence must be prompt and cost-efficient. Since these are attributes of primary research on the Internet, businesses benefit from access to customers worldwide. Examples of topics that can beneficially be researched on the Internet include customer satisfaction, product concept generation, and usability testing.

A focus group on the Internet can be used to gather information about a specific problem. Participants in a focus group have equal opportunity to supply answers to the question(s) asked and to express their points of view. After setting up a focus group on the Net, one or more questions can be asked of the Internet user. A question might be: "What is the biggest problem you have had with the widget?" Customers' answers to this question will be analyzed by marketers in searching for solutions that will assure a more rewarding experience for the customers. A drawback to online focus groups is that the participants may not identify themselves truthfully. For example, a 16-year-old male could identify himself as a 35-year-old housewife.

Among the steps recommended by Vassos (1996) in conducting primary research on the Internet are:

- Define the target market.
- Identify the discussion groups in which the target market might be participating.
- Identify the topics under discussion.
- Search UseNet and e-mail discussion group topic lists and content to find the target market.
- Subscribe to appropriate UseNet and e-mail discussion groups and post question(s).

In addition to primary research, the marketer can save time and money by conducting secondary research on the Internet when the information needed has already been compiled by other organizations or government agencies. Internet search engines facilitate sorting quickly through enormous amounts of information. Examples of information available on the Internet through secondary research include population demographic statistics (search on words such as census, demographics, and population), the national trade data bank, and U. S. trademarks and patents. Knowing the trademarks and patents that are current, a company can avoid applying for a duplicate and refrain from infringing on another company's patent. To locate a specific article in a specified publication, the researcher can start at Newslink, which has links to more than 3,000 publications.

The Internet can also be a source of competitive information. Marketers can monitor competitors' movements and possibly their intentions by reading and studying information on home pages, reviewing annual reports, and examining postings to newsgroups. The possibilities also include getting competitive pricing information and press release data.

By analyzing competitor organizations' mission statements found on the Internet, marketers may revise their own mission statement to be more descriptive of their company's marketing activities. Another name for a mission statement (strategic focus, strategy, or corporate goals and objectives) may also result from an Internet search of other companies' mission statements.

Major demographic trends (age, sex, race, income, occupation, geographic location) are important to marketers because people make up markets. The numbers of people in a demographic category can show the size of markets. Internet searches on the following topics or titles will provide important data for analyzing potential markets: census, USA Statistics in Brief, the World Factbook, CIA Publications, and state rankings and vital statistics for identified states.

Assessing market potential is essential when marketing a specific product or service. A target market should be large enough to assure profits. Online databases on the Internet can provide marketers with information to determine if markets are substantial.

By engaging in market research on the Internet, marketers can interact more directly with their customers, a tremendous benefit since customers *are* the market. Additionally, marketers can engage in primary and secondary research about their competitors, potential markets, and the regulatory environment, thus avoiding the limitations of traditional research methods. Understanding the value of doing market research on the Internet and looking into the future will give marketers the competitive advantage needed to be effective in the 21st century.

International Marketing

The Internet has changed international trade. This medium helps to level the playing field of competition by allowing both small and large companies to access the Internet. The Internet somewhat reduces the competitive advantage of the large companies and makes it easier for small companies to compete worldwide.

Access to the Internet has grown faster in the United States than in countries abroad. However, as online services become aggressive in marketing their services, Internet access abroad is expected to grow rapidly. In addition, foreign national governments are showing more interest in the Internet, though some governments are likely to resist the free flow of ideas that is characteristic of the Internet.

Expanding access to the Internet means expanding markets, including finding markets for new products and developing new products. By discovering international markets and determining national preferences, marketers can customize products to the desires of the consumers in a specific country. For example, a U.S.-based book publisher can upload chapters from selected books in several languages for Internet users worldwide to sample. Reading these chapters in the native language creates a demand for the books, thus expanding the market.

Rapid information flow internationally requires marketers to develop an awareness of the potential for a variety of crises. News of cross-border differences in price, quality, and availability will be difficult, if not impossible, to suppress. Discounts offered in one country but withheld in another could easily lead to a crisis. Thus, marketers must consider carefully all postings on the Internet since the information will be disseminated very rapidly and will reach the entire world.

MARKETING-RELATED WEB SITES. Below are examples of marketing-related Web sites.

- American Marketing Association

     http://www.ama.org/hmpage.htm

- Web Trends

     http://future.sri.com/vals/valshome.html

- Top Businesses in a Geographic Market Area

     http://www.toplist.com

- Market Industry Reports

     http://www.findsypcom

- Marketing Research Firms

     http://www.gallup.com

     http://www.nielsen.com

     http://www.teleport.com/ ~ tbchad/stats1.html

- Marketing Research on the Net

     http://www.survey.net

Internet Issues and Concerns

Information on how to access and use the Internet is continuously proclaimed by word-of-mouth, advertising, and all forms of broadcast and print media. Readers of newspapers, magazines, journals, and other printed materials receive invitations to "visit our Web site." Television advertising often ends with a WWW address for viewer use. Maloff (1996) describes the Internet as "daily fodder for newspapers, television, and radio." Attendant to this fodder are implications for business users that require careful consideration, such as the issues and concerns expressed below. The business users of the Internet should carefully consider these issues.

Perhaps the most serious issue for Internet usage is that of security and the lack of planning for security. The Internet is an unprotected medium where information flows are open to perusal by anyone, thus rendering sensitive and valuable information vulnerable to misappropriation by criminals. Business organizations must plan for security, submit the plan in writing, disseminate the written plan, and update the plan regularly.

Security threats originate from inside the company as well as from outside the company. Firewalls, passwords, encryption, and user authentication are some of the means used to achieve network security. Maloff (1996) suggests building network security "like layers of an onion." When invaders (hackers) break through one area, they should encounter another hindrance to access. Realizing that no telecommunications medium is totally secure, businesses can develop acceptable network security with knowledgeable, thoughtful planning.

Accessing the Internet includes not only giving business personnel the privilege of using the Internet, but also being able to actually access Internet sites. The results of a Conference Board questionnaire on corporate use of the Internet revealed that while 82 percent of the companies surveyed had access to the Internet, not all employees of those companies were granted this privilege. Of the companies reporting Internet access, 74 percent reported that the Internet was not available for all employees. Lack of access was due to requirements of management approval, limitations of network/hardware/support systems, and limitations on applications (Conference Board, 1996).

A second problem with access is the overcrowded condition of the Internet. When millions of users access the Net, delays of several minutes to several hours occur. Although understandable, these delays are irritating and costly. For businesses, the Internet yields the advantages of easier access and less wait time for out-of-prime-time usage. Unfortunately, inability to access the Internet has created questions about its usefulness: If a company cannot access the Internet when it needs to do so, why be connected?

The attitudes and approaches of some key company personnel towards the Internet reveal their current concerns regarding its usage. Believing that it is only a fad and refusing to accept its potential, some company officials are reluctant to connect to the Net. These doubters may admit that a Web site for

eir company could be exciting, but they are not convinced that use of the
et could increase productivity or bring in new customers. A question
pically asked is: "How many of our customers actually use the Net?"

The absence of a thoughtful, well-developed plan for Internet use may
dicate that an organization has used a gut-feel approach based on establish-
g its Internet connection "because we need to" or "because everyone is
oing it." Consultants and planners recommend the following problem-
olving process:

- Determine company expectations for Internet usage.
- Identify company personnel to be involved.
- Suggest alternatives.

This approach should ensure more reliable business decisions based on
otential opportunities assessed, risks and investments involved, and benefits
xpected.

Personnel positions and assignments pose another concern for company
management. One example is that the potential for direct sales on the Internet
ould reduce the need for sales agents in businesses such as real estate, insur-
nce, and banking, who will have been relegated to the role of middlemen.

The approach to selecting employees to oversee Internet strategy within a
ompany often signifies the commitment a company has made to the Internet.
ome executives view the Internet strategy as a part-time duty and thus
ecommend that this responsibility be assigned as an add-on to the duties of
nother employee who might be employed in the management information
ystem unit of the company. Administering an Internet connection, however, is
full-time responsibility requiring technical expertise and appreciation of the
mplications for using the Internet throughout the company. Further, consult-
nts suggest that administering the Internet must be important enough to be
udgeted properly. Maintaining a once-established Internet site is an ongoing,
ynamic job and must be adequately funded and staffed.

Actually, establishing an Internet connection may require the addition of
n Internet resource executive. This position is not strictly technical; the
osition requires experience in marketing, networking, the Internet, strategic
lanning, and an understanding of the firm's mission. The person in this
osition works with all the units within the organization in attempting to
oordinate and promote activities on the Internet. The Internet resource
xecutive occupies a unique position from which to ensure that the divisions
f a business organization share resources resulting in cost savings. While
ach division within an organization must have the autonomy to pursue its
wn objectives, all divisions need to work cooperatively when developing the
ompany-wide Internet site.

A serious handicap of the Internet itself is its lack of organization. Most
usinesspersons want to know who is in charge of activities or events. In
eference to the Internet, no one is in charge since no one owns the Internet.

No one controls it, and no one is responsible for its reliability. Many business and non-business individuals are concerned about this characteristic of the Internet.

Although many issues and concerns accompany the growing commercial use of the Internet, it remains a vital and expanding ingredient in the way companies large and small conduct their business. Management and marketing executives are successfully taking advantage of the Internet's capabilities, and educators at all levels are also enhancing their teaching activities through Internet usage.

102

Using the Internet in Business Education

Along with managers and marketers, business educators and students have risen to the challenges and opportunities offered by the Internet. However, lack of funds for acquiring the necessary hardware and software often limit access to the Internet for all students in a classroom setting. By the year 2000, the goal of the Clinton administration is to have all the nation's schools and libraries connected to the Internet.

Once access is attained, educators can focus on incorporating into student learning activities and information that is both current and derived from worldwide resources. Potential uses of the Internet in classroom settings are limited only by the imagination and creativity of the teacher.

Use of the Internet requires and improves upon a number of skills including verbal, written, critical thinking, computer, and telecommunications. Additional benefits of Internet use include making learning exciting and fun, providing unlimited information, and encouraging cooperative learning, collaborative projects, and idea sharing.

Additionally, the Internet provides teachers with several classroom benefits:

- Obtaining current information on topics for the classes they teach.
- Sharing lesson plans, curriculum ideas, and software with other educators.
- Making lesson planning more productive.
- Increasing student motivation.

Specifically, for management and marketing teachers, the Internet offers many activities incorporating the following concepts: communication, global environment, research, career exploration, planning, workforce diversity, and ethics and social responsibility.

Specific activities include the following:

- Send e-mail locally and abroad.
- Visit a Fortune 500 company Web site and report selected information to instructor.

- Research companies and explain how they are moving to globalize their management structure.

- Design an online resume.

- Use online job centers to find companies in which students are interested.

- Plan a home page for personal use or for a specific organization.

- Determine the age, gender, and ethnic origin of the people in a specific town or region.

- Research and write a report on the social responsibility of individuals and/or businesses.

When access is available, energetic, enthusiastic teachers will create many valuable activities for student motivation and enjoyment. Both students and teachers will benefit — as learning is enhanced and as interest in the Internet increases.

BUSINESS EDUCATION-RELATED WEB SITES. Listed below are examples of business education-related Web sites.

- The Purdue Online Writing Lab

    http://owl.trc.purdue.edu/by-topic-alternate.html

- The Virtual Law Library

    http://www.law.indiana.edu/law/lawindex.html

- Communications

    http://www.smartbiz.com/sbs/cats/comm.htm

- International Law

    http://www.noord.bart.nl/ ~ bethlelhem/law.html

- WEB — Entrepreneurship Education Resources

    http://www.slu.edu/eweb

- Multinational Companies on the Net

    http://web.idirect.com/ ~ tiger/worldbea.htm

- Employment Opportunities and Job Resources

    http://www.dbm.com/jobguide

- Netiquette Home Page

    http://rs6000.adm.fau.edu/rinaldi/netiquette.html

- Employment/Career Mosaic

    http://www.careermosaic.com

- America's Job Bank

    http://www.ajb.dni.us/index.html

Summary

The Internet assists businesses in meeting the demands of competition in today's broadened, global economy. Innovative, enterprising marketing and management personnel can be leaders in their firms by developing cyberspace activities designed to increase markets, to improve customer relations, and to provide information for decision-making.

The constantly changing nature of the Internet requires diligence in establishing and maintaining a viable presence on the Internet. A home page, properly constructed and maintained, can effectively promote business interests on the Internet through the exchange of information between businesses and their customers.

As a communication tool the Internet has no equal. E-mail, the most widely used of all Internet services, provides an easy, convenient, and cost-effective communication method. Businesses expect their personnel to use e-mail effectively and to cope with the information load accompanying its use.

Marketers can use the Internet as a public relations tool. Individual, direct contact with customers allows the marketer to address specific customer questions and/or concerns. Participating in discussion groups discloses customer questions, complaints, and topics of customer interest that the marketer can then address.

Primary research on the Internet in regard to customer satisfaction, concept generation, and usability testing permits marketers to obtain current information. Specific problems may be addressed by posing a particular question of interest to marketers and analyzing customers' answers.

Secondary research through Internet search engines allows marketers to gather information on population demographic statistics, the national trade bank, and trademarks and patents. Competitive information, major demographic trends, and market potential may also be researched on the Internet.

The Internet provides international access to potential customers for both small and large companies. Expanding access means enlarging markets for new products and for developing new markets.

Internet use, however, uncovers a number of issues. These concerns include security and the lack of planning for security; access to the Internet for more employees, educators, and students; attitudes and approaches to the Internet by key personnel; absence of a well-developed plan for Internet use; and Internet personnel positions and assignments. A very serious issue with the Internet itself is the lack of organization, or, stated another way, "Who's in charge of the Internet?"

Business educators can benefit from the Internet by obtaining current information on classes taught, sharing classroom-related ideas, and increasing student motivation. Among the class activities teachers may use are designing an online resume, sending and receiving e-mail, and planning a home page for personal use.

The Internet is not a fad and will not disappear. This electronic medium offers challenges and opportunities, as well as solutions to many business and education problems. Businesses and business teachers willing to embrace new and future challenges, to take risks, and to support new thinking will survive and succeed in the information revolution.

105

References

Business, Technology, and the Internet (Conference Board Rep. No. 1143-96-CR). (1996). USA: Conference Board.

Hall, G., and Allen, G. (1996). *The Internet Guide for Marketing.* Cincinnati, OH: South-Western.

Peshin, C. B. (1997). *Management on the World Wide Web.* Upper Saddle River, NJ: Prentice Hall.

Maloff, J. (1996, November). Do Execs Get the Net? *Internet World,* 7(11), 64-68.

Vassos, T. (1996). *Strategic Internet Marketing.* Indianapolis, IN: Que.

Chapter 10 — Integrating the Internet Into a Methods Class

by Margaret J. Erthal
Southern Illinois University — Edwardsville, Illinois

Much has been written about the history and uses of the Internet and its potential to change the way we learn and interact with the world (Levine and Baroudi, 1994; Ellsworth, 1994; Brown, 1996; Crockett and Hall, 1997). The stakeholders include businesses, government, agencies, and education, and each group intends to utilize the Internet to improve its competitive advantage in the marketplace. Businesses hope to advertise their products and services to virtual clients, thus, increasing their profits. Governments at the state and national levels are ready to disseminate information to the citizens. Agencies can solicit for funds and create awareness of social issues. Educational institutions are scrambling to obtain Internet connections in their schools and then use the World Wide Web to enhance and supplement the learning environment. Schools, and teachers specifically, are being held responsible for providing Internet instruction, and parents expect this tool for their children.

The intent of this chapter is to explore Internet integration within the business education methods class. Broad areas, such as communications, curriculum, lesson planning, and evaluation are discussed. Lastly, the *National Standards for Business Education* (1995) published by the National Business Education Association (NBEA) are linked to the Internet, and selected Internet-related standards with activities are listed.

Communications

Communications may be spoken or written and, depending on the medium, may be more or less efficient. For example, telephone tag is less efficient than electronic communications. However, if the recipient does not utilize electronic communications, then that form is useless. Electronic communications in the business education methods class consists of three basic types: electronic mail, or e-mail, discussion groups also referred to as listservs, and the home page.

E-MAIL. Perhaps the most frequent Internet use is devoted to e-mail. E-mail offers users the benefits of sending and receiving mail but at the user's convenience. Students enjoy e-mail and immediately begin to send and receive messages. Assignments include sending a message, replying to a message, and forwarding a message. An address book relieves the tedious, repetitive keying of a recipient's e-mail address. Students not only create individual addresses, but also a mailing list that allows them to broadcast a message. Depending on the communications software, attachments are utilized to decrease paper handling. It is advantageous for business education methods students to utilize more than one e-mail package such as Pine, Eudora, and e-mail packages associated with Web browsers such as Netscape. Not only can students boast of competence in packages, but they can experience transfer of knowledge and training.

DISCUSSION GROUPS AND LISTSERVS. Students should be exposed to various points of view by joining and participating in electronic discussions such as a listserv. A listserv is a network-based discussion group devoted to one topic (Wagner, 1996). It is an automated mailing list of people with similar interests (Wagner, 1995). The subscription is free and may be canceled at any time. An essential listserv for prospective business education teachers is VOCNET, which is sponsored by the National Center for Research in Vocational Education (NCRVE). This listserv is a forum for the exchange of topics of interest to all vocational teachers such as current trends, legislative issues, upcoming conferences, employment opportunities, etc. Two additional, useful listservs include BATECH-L for Technologies in Business Education and BUSED-L, which discuss business education teaching practices. In order for students to gain maximum exposure, they are encouraged to respond to a topic of interest and/or pose a question. When the topic appears to be "dead," a summary of the discussion follows and is shared with peers (Wagner, 1995; Wagner, 1996; Ellsworth, 1994; Levine and Baroudi, 1994). Instructions for joining a listserv are included in Table 1.

HOME PAGE. A teacher-developed home page can provide students with the syllabus and internal and external links that point to additional resources. As students gain familiarity with the Internet, they are required to develop their own home page and upload it to a server using File Transfer Protocol (FTP). As the course progresses, students download their home page, perform editing to reflect changes, and upload the new product. Minimum home page requirements include: background color, graphic images, internal and external links, and an e-mail reference. In addition to teacher-developed home pages, educational institutions, the government, and various organizations have home pages on the Internet. Teachers and individuals seem to have their favorites and are encouraged to share Internet addresses with their peers. Specific home pages that are beneficial to prospective business education teachers are the National Business Education Association; U.S. Department of Education, Office of

108

Table 1: Listserv Addresses*

To subscribe to a list service, e-mail a message to the indicated address. Remove any signature information and in the body type: subscribe firstname lastname.

BATECH-L	Technologies in Business Education	batech-l@psuvm.psu.edu
BUSED-L	Discussion of Business Education Teaching Practices	bused-l@ureginal.bitnet
NBEA	National Business Education Association	nbea-l@akronvm.bitnet
STWNET	School-to-Work International Gateway	majordomo@confer.edc.org
VOCNET	National Center for Research in Vocational Education	vocnet@cmsa.berkeley.edu

*Addresses may change from time to time.

Vocational and Adult Education; School-to-Work Gateway; and the National Center for Research in Vocational Education. These home pages represent a method for business education teachers to stay abreast of current trends, legislation, conferences, and issues. URL addresses are listed in Table 2.

Curriculum

A curriculum designer without Internet access is sorely limited, especially in the business education discipline. Being cognizant of current workplace trends and issues and proposed legislative agendas is where the Internet shines. From SCANS to School-to-Work legislation to computer software, the Internet serves as the Information Superhighway. Beginning teachers are not always well-versed in curriculum development and tend to teach what the book offers. Good curriculum resources are the National Business Education Association (NBEA) Standards and Educational Resources Information Center (ERIC). An important point to impress upon students is the fact that anyone can post to the Internet; therefore, the topic could be one person's opinion and possibly not as reliable or useful as other sources might be. It is the educator's responsibility to share respected journal titles with the students.

ACCOUNTING. The Internet allows accounting students to speak with professionals in the field and access national organizations' publications. As students prepare a curriculum, they are at the cutting edge of the discipline. In addition to using objectives from the text, students can review curriculum objectives from all over the world. Chat rooms and frequently asked questions (FAQ) are sources of conversation and views related to accounting topics. In addition, prospective teachers have access to research through professional journals.

CONSUMER EDUCATION. A wealth of curriculum resources awaits the consumer education teacher via the Internet. Current social, political, and legal issues can be identified and addressed to add relevancy to any course. Public domain software and shareware simulations are available and can be downloaded free or for a nominal charge. This software allows students to apply concepts related to credit, insurance, budgeting, retirement, investments, etc. The *Consumer Resource Handbook* is now available on disk and may be shared with students. This valuable resource includes names, addresses, and phone numbers of consumer agencies. Students are required to locate a shareware package related to a consumer topic, download the program, and investigate the usefulness of the program and provide a summary to their peers.

GENERAL BUSINESS. In order for schools to prepare students for life in a global economy, teachers must be cognizant of national and international business standards. Curriculum development in general business is enhanced by the Internet. Entrepreneurship can be researched through the Small Business Administration's Web site, and students can explore entrepreneurship activities across the nation. International culture and etiquette are a first step in understanding other customs, and this information is available on the Internet. Students

Table 2: URL Addresses*

- Classroom Connect
  - http://www.classroom.net
- Search Engine Directory
  - http://www.library.nwu.edu/resources/Internet/search/evaluate.html
- Area Maps
  - http://www.mapquest.com
  - http://www.tripquest.com
- Shareware
  - http://www.shareware.com
- Curriculum
  - http://www.ericir.syr.edu
- Travel
  - http://www.travelcity.com
- International Business
  - http://www.hmco.com/hmco/school/ss/links/ss_5.html
  - http://www.worldweb.net/~berriss/
- Small Business Administration
  - http://www.sbaonline.sba.gov/
- National Center for Research in Vocational Education
  - http://www.ncrve.berkeley.edu
- School-to-Work
  - http://www.stw.edu.gov
- Search Engines
  - http://www.altavista.digital.com
  - http://www.lycos.com
  - http://www.infoseek.com
  - http://www.yahoo.com
- U.S. Department of Education
  - http://www.ed.gov

*Addresses may change from time to time.

plan for a trip to another country and must research that country's customs, language, and culture, in addition, to determining currency exchange rates.

BUSINESS COMMUNICATIONS. The Internet is all about communicating and provides users with endless possibilities. Teachers can design curricula by utilizing online writing labs and sending students on a virtual literary scavenger hunt. Students begin writing electronic good news, bad news, and persuasive messages. These same messages are evaluated and the results returned electronically. Collaborative writing projects are assigned with classroom peers and peers around the world. Students download a graphic image that represents their logo and use it throughout the term on every piece of communication.

111

MARKETING. Changes in marketing components, such as advertising, retailing, and research, can be quickly incorporated into curriculum development via the Internet. Virtual advertising is in place and students can explore and experience this profitable medium. The competition's strategies can be assessed and evaluated as students design and implement an advertising campaign. Students trace the development of a new product and then disseminate the information to their peers. An organization's marketing plan may be identified, thoroughly examined, and then compared with similar industries.

INFORMATION PROCESSING. The broad area of information processing is probably the easiest in which to integrate the Internet. An office systems curriculum should reflect current technology and human resource issues, which are available and up-to-date via the Internet. The ideas for integration are endless when designing a computer applications curriculum. In addition to teaching the technology, students can be exposed to alternate word processing, spreadsheet, database, and presentation graphics software packages. Keyboarding drill and practice software, similar to popular and expensive packages, can be downloaded from shareware sites.

Lesson Planning

After designing the course curriculum, objectives and activities become the impetus for daily lesson plans. While objectives are the starting point for curriculum planning, behavioral objectives are the basis for daily lesson planning.

OBJECTIVES. A well-planned objective includes conditions, terminal behavior, and criteria. Conditions include the "givens," while terminal behavior specifies what the learner should be able to do, and criteria establish evaluation in the areas of time and accuracy. Instead of: "After reading Chapter 4, the learner will be able to identify four financial institutions with 90 percent accuracy in 30 minutes," the objective could be: "After researching the Internet, the learner will be able to identify and download four articles related to financial institutions with 90 percent accuracy in 30 minutes." Helping the prospective teacher explore the Internet is interwoven into methods class objectives. The teacher will need frequent Internet access to ascertain new developments in a discipline so that objectives will reflect current trends.

ACTIVITIES. Carefully structured activities to supplement lesson planning are still necessary. Trying to explain the sound of waves breaking on the beach is difficult. However, a student experiencing the sound of waves breaking on the beach via the Internet might be the next best thing to being there. The Internet can provide immediate feedback instead of the student getting a paper returned the next day. The Internet also allows students to work at their own rate and explore tangent topics. Paper/pencil activities may be replaced by Internet activities, and cooperative learning activities may be integrated just as they would be in a traditional classroom. Students teach th technology as a cooperative learning activity (Kizzier, 1995) after installing an appropriate software package downloaded from a shareware Internet site.

Evaluation

Evaluation provides the students and the teacher with an opportunity to assess learning. Students can identify knowledge gaps and progress in meeting objectives, while teachers can ascertain if their instructional delivery methods are effective. Internet usage still dictates that evaluation occurs in order to measure the objectives.

PORTFOLIOS. A recent trend has been for learners to assemble a collection of their progress to show an employer, teacher, counselor, or supervisor. Rather than tell someone you can aptly "surf the net," you can exhibit your products in the form of hardcopy printouts and/or files down-loaded to disk. A useful activity is to e-mail students a series of questions that requires Internet use to answer. Not only does this activity contribute to portfolio development, it requires problem-solving skills and helps students refine their search techniques.

AUTHENTIC ASSESSMENT. Closely related to portfolio development is authentic assessment, which is a performance-based evaluation tool. Instead of asking students to list the necessary steps to log on to their e-mail accounts have them send you an e-mail message. Authentic assessment may also be used to assess higher-level abilities at the analysis, synthesis, and evaluation levels of Bloom's Taxonomy. For example, students could be required to use four different search engines to determine the one most suited for the task. In order to find information, a search engine should be utilized, which allows the student to be more efficient when "surfing the net." Popular search engines are listed in Table 2. By carefully structuring activities, authentic assessment is a viable alternative to traditional evaluation tools.

National Standards for Business Education

During 1995, the *National Standards for Business Education* became available to all business educators. This document provides benchmarks for teachers from elementary to postsecondary schools to determine what students should know and be able to do. The following sections illustrate selected National Business Education Association Standards as they apply to Internet usage in the business education methods class.

ACCOUNTING. The achievement standard for financial statements is: ". . . interpret and analyze financial statements . . . for service, merchandising, and manufacturing businesses" (*National Standards for Business Education*, 1995, p. 18). Using the Internet, students could locate the appropriate

ancial statements for the three types of businesses (proprietorship, partner-
ip, and corporation) and perform analysis and interpretation on the finan-
al statements. The achievement standard for interpretation and use of data
". . . evaluate the performance of an organization and apply differential
alysis and present value concepts to make decisions" (*National Standards for
usiness Education*, 1995, p. 20). Using the above-mentioned various financial
atements, students could apply this achievement standard by comparing
ganizations' monetary values.

113

ECONOMICS AND PERSONAL FINANCE. The achievement standard
r personal decision-making is: "Use a rational decision-making process
it applies to the roles of citizens, workers, and consumers" (*National
andards for Business Education*, 1995, p. 62). Given a problem dealing
ith economic decision-making, students could use the Internet to locate
cts and arrive at a plausible alternative to a problem. The achievement
andard for the role of government is: "Discuss the . . . necessary and
sirable role of government in the U.S. economy" (*National Standards for
usiness Education*, 1995, p. 73). Students could be given scenarios and
en use the Internet to solve the problem of too much or too little govern-
ent intervention and the effect on society. The achievement standard for
e role of citizens is: "Describe the rights and responsibilities of citizens in
e U.S. economy, including their role in making decisions through the
litical process. . . ." After searching the Internet, students should be able
establish cause and effect when given political choices and issues, such
building a hospital or repairing the infrastructure.

ENTREPRENEURSHIP. The achievement standard for entrepreneurship
aracteristics is: "Identify unique characteristics of an entrepreneur and evaluate
e degree to which one possesses those characteristics" (*National Standards for
usiness Education*, 1995, p. 78). Using various search engines, students could
cate entrepreneurs and identify common traits and then determine if these
aits match theirs. The achievement standard for entrepreneurship business
ans is: "Develop a business plan" (*National Standards for Business Education*,
995, p. 90). By reviewing entrepreneur business plans on the Internet, students
uld begin developing a business plan in order to obtain financing.

INTERNATIONAL BUSINESS. The achievement standard for
ternational business awareness is: "Explain the role of international
usiness and analyze its impact on careers and doing business at the local,
ate, national, and international levels" (*National Standards for Business
ducation*, 1995, p. 102). Researching through the Internet could identify
usinesses that have international customers and possible employment
portunities and criteria. The achievement standard for organizational
ructure of international businesses is: "Identify forms of business ownership
d entrepreneurial opportunities available in international business"
National Standards for Business Education, 1995, p. 113). Students could
etermine if one particular form of business ownership is more closely
igned with international business by researching the Internet.

COMMUNICATIONS. The achievement standard for technological communications is: "Use technology to enhance the effectiveness of communications" (*National Standards for Business Education*, 1995, p. 51). Using electronic communications, students could describe how to assemble a widget and send the documentation to a peer. The recipient could then follow the directions to check for accuracy. The achievement standard for employment communications is: "Integrate all forms of communication in the successful pursuit of a career" (*National Standards for Business Education*, 1995, p. 52). Opportunities for Internet use are endless in this instance. Not only could students review employment opportunities, but they could post their resumes on the Internet.

MARKETING. The achievement standard for the roles of marketing is: "Identify the roles of marketing and analyze the impact of marketing on the individual, business, and society" (*National Standards for Business Education*, 1995, p. 128). Students could analyze the ethical or non-ethical behavior of firms and determine the effect on employees, the community, and society. The achievement standard for characteristics of a market is: "Identify numerous marketing variables and strategies in dealing with a diversified marketplace" (*National Standards for Business Education*, 1995, p. 134). Students could develop a fictitious product and use the Internet to identify possible markets.

INFORMATION SYSTEMS. The achievement standard for information systems planning and acquisition is: "Plan the selection and acquisition of information systems" (*National Standards for Business Education*, 1995, p. 96). Students may contact vendors and manufacturers to acquire an information system that meets predetermined criteria. The achievement standard for the social and economic impact of information systems is: "Assess the impact of information systems on society" (*National Standards for Business Education*, 1995, p. 98). Students could select one facet of an information system, such as order processing completed manually and electronically, and then determine the effect on employees, the organization, and vendors.

Summary

The Internet is here to stay and those who can utilize it most effectively and efficiently will be in demand in business, government, and education. It is essential that prospective business education teachers have a firm grasp of the Internet and be able to integrate this technology into the classroom. One role of the business educator is to design, develop, implement, and evaluate Internet activities that will allow prospective teachers to become truly computer and Internet literate. The business education methods class is an ideal vehicle to allow prospective business teachers to become familiar with the Internet, explore its potential, and investigate its possibilities.

References

Amlin, R. (1995). *Teaching the Internet*. [Online]. Available: http://www.mvhs.edu/tech/CUE_article.html.

rown, H. (1996). *A Guide for Using the Internet*. Little Rock, AR: Delta Pi Epsilon.

llsworth, J. (1994). *Education on the Internet*. Indianapolis: Sam's Publishing.

latley, M. (1996). *Teaching Electronic Communications: Technology for the Digital Age*. Little Rock, AR: Delta Pi Epsilon.

latley, M. and Hunter, J. (1995). Electronic Mail, Bulletin Board Systems, Conferences: Connections for the Electronic Teaching/Learning Age. In N. Groneman (Ed.), *Technology in the Classroom: 1995 NBEA Yearbook, No. 33* (pp. 73-85). Reston, VA: National Business Education Association.

ill, R. (1996). *Internet Ahead!* Speech presented at the St. Louis Area Business Education Association Meeting. St. Louis, MO.

lall, G. and Crockett, H. (1997). *Netscape 2: Projects for the Internet*. Menlo Park, CA: The Benjamin/Cummings Publishing Company, Inc.

mel, S., Kerka, S., and Wagner, J. (1996). *Demystifying the Internet and Untangling the Web*. ERIC Clearinghouse on Adult, Career, and Vocational Education. Columbus, OH: Ohio State University.

iaderstrom, S. (1995). Technology's Impact on Computer and Business Curricula. In N. Groneman (Ed.), *Technology in the Classroom: 1995 NBEA Yearbook, No. 33* (pp. 1-9). Reston, VA: National Business Education Association.

iizzier, D. (1995). Teaching Technology vs. Technology as a Teaching Tool. In N. Groneman (Ed.), *Technology in the Classroom: 1995 NBEA Yearbook, No. 33* (pp. 10-24). Reston, VA: National Business Education Association.

evine, J. and Baroudi, C. (1994). *The Internet for Dummies* (2nd ed.). San Mateo, CA: IDG Books Worldwide, Inc.

latyska, R. (1995, December). *Integrating the Internet Into the Business Education Classroom*. Roundtable session presentation at the meeting of the American Vocational Association.

lational Business Education Association. (1995). *National Standards for Business Education: What American Students Should Know and Be Able to Do in Business*. Reston, VA: National Business Education Association.

lational Business Education Association. (In press). *Business Teacher Education Curriculum Guide and Program Standards*. Reston, VA: National Business Education Association.

Vagner, J. (1995). *Using the Internet in Vocational Education*. [Online]. Available: http://www.osu.edu/units/education/cete/ericacve/do14cs/Internet.htm.

Vagner, J. (1996). *Locating Vocational Education Curriculum and Instructional Materials*. ERIC Clearinghouse on Adult, Career and Vocational Education. Columbus, OH: Ohio State University.

Chapter 11 — Internet Use in Document Processing and Computer Applications

by Dennis Boldt
Hillsboro High School — Hillsboro, Kansas
and
Nancy Groneman
Emporia State University — Emporia, Kansas

As Internet availability in schools grows, educators must prepare themselves to apply this valuable resource to their courses. In many instances, business instructors are responsible for computer applications courses, as well as traditional business courses. As business instructors, we must utilize the Internet as a resource tool. As computer instructors, we must not only utilize the Internet as a tool, but also instruct the proper usage of computer software that allows interaction with the Internet.

As Internet usage grows more common, students will enter school with knowledge of computer functions such as loading and working with a browser, searching for information, and downloading text and graphics. Currently, students enter middle schools and high schools with different levels of Internet proficiency. Even though computers in the home are becoming more and more common, many students first encounter the Internet at school. Teachers must prepare for this variance in proficiency when planning lessons.

The Internet is quickly turning into one of the most valuable tools in education. In business departments, teachers can use the Internet to communicate with others in their field and to conduct research. Students can use it as a tool to locate information, as well as to communicate with other students and with business employees around the world. The potential of the Internet is endless.

Students are drawn to the possibilities the Internet offers; however, we must be selective in the material used in our classrooms. The Internet is invaluable in raising students' interest, and this justifies applying it to our courses. The Internet contains a vast amount of information available to anyone with a computer and an Internet connection, but is viewed by many as simply a mode of entertainment or a source of meaningless information. It is our responsibility as educators to seek valuable information on the Internet and apply it in a positive, instructional manner in our classrooms.

Controlling Internet Access

118

One of the first steps before allowing students access to the Internet should be the creation of an Acceptable Use Policy. Those who have spent any time using the Internet realize the vast amount of material available that is inappropriate in a school setting.

Each school district must take into consideration where computers are to be located and how much supervision will be available to monitor Internet usage. Will the computers that are capable of accessing the Internet be located in the classroom, in a supervised laboratory, or in a laboratory that does not have constant supervision? The amount of supervision in areas utilizing the Internet is one important consideration in an Acceptable Use Policy (AUP). For a complete discussion on developing an AUP, see Chapters 2 and 3.

The amount of Internet supervision will also determine if software that provides a firewall is necessary on a school's computer system. The term firewall refers to software that prevents users from accessing certain addresses on the Internet. This software can be programmed to eliminate access to all addresses containing a specific domain such as those with *.com* extensions, or *.org* extensions. This type of software can also be programmed to eliminate access to individual addresses or can allow access to only addresses selected by the teacher.

Denying access to all addresses with one specific domain will eliminate a great number of sites. This may not be what the classroom teacher desires. For example, many sites not suitable for educational purposes can be found on commercial sites. These sites contain the extension *.com* in the address. This does not mean that all sites with *.com* extensions are inappropriate for educational purposes. Instead of eliminating all commercial sites, the software can be programmed to eliminate access to specific addresses. Although no firewall can eliminate all controversial material, appropriate software can minimize inappropriate access.

Hundreds of new Web sites are added to the Internet daily. Assessing the appropriateness of sites takes a great deal of time and is one reason firewall software alone will not solve the problem of inappropriate access. It is important to utilize proper instruction prior to access, as well as maintaining teacher supervision.

Ways to Integrate Internet Usage

The following section describes the goals of a one semester document processing course and a one semester computer applications course and the ways that Internet usage can be integrated into those courses. These courses are required at Hillsboro High School in Hillsboro, Kansas, and generally

fered to 10th grade level students with the document processing course
ken first. An advanced document processing and computer applications
urse are recommended electives after the required courses have been
mpleted.

cument Processing I

The course description for Document Processing I follows:

*Document Processing I is designed to define the basic keyboarding and
formatting skills learned at the elementary and middle school levels.
The primary objective is to instruct students in the usage of a word
processing software package in order to create production documents
such as tables, outlines, reports, and correspondence including notes,
memos, and letters. Students will also be introduced to a presentation
software package such as PowerPoint and receive instruction on
accessing and utilizing the Internet.*

As required business courses, students must complete specific outcomes
ring each semester. All departmental outcomes are aligned with district
tcomes. Two district outcomes that align with the business department
als are (1) to prepare students to be adaptable technologists, and (2) to
epare students to be information users. The Internet provides an avenue
ading toward both goals.

As stated in the course description, the primary objective of the Docu-
ent Processing I course is to teach keyboarding and formatting skills. Since
yboarding is now introduced at the elementary school level, students now
ter high school with a high keyboarding proficiency, allowing more time for
struction on utilizing computer software, including software used for access-
g the Internet.

In Document Processing I, students receive instruction on the proper
rmatting of a variety of correspondence including term and research papers.
Hillsboro High School, the business and English departments collaborate in
dent research paper instruction during the first semester of the school year.
e collaboration involves a great deal of communication between depart-
ents. At Hillsboro High School, the majority of students enrolled in English
are also enrolled in Document Processing I. In many ways, this utilizes the
ncept of team teaching. Both teachers are involved and work together to
sist students in creating a research paper required for both classes. Conflict-
g class schedules and class sizes do not allow teachers from both depart-
ents to be in the same classroom during the instruction. Students are
quired to key and format research papers in Document Processing I. In this
urse, students' word processing and formatting skills are evaluated from
search assignments that began in the English courses.

The collaboration between the business and English departments helps
dents make better use of their time and allows them to receive manuscript
struction from both departments to help create well-organized papers.

Collaborative efforts allow students to utilize computer lab time in order to complete research papers. Students are encouraged to use the Internet as a resource tool to find information about their topics. In order to prepare students to use the Internet as a resource tool, Internet instruction is approached in the following sequence:

- Students are taught how to use current browser software to access Internet sites. This browser software could include Netscape, Microsoft Explorer, Mosaic, or others.

- Students are shown how to find sites for information using a search engine such as Web Crawler, Lycos, Infoseek, Magellan or any of the many available search engines.

- Students are taught methods to download and print information using the hardware available in the computer classroom or laborator

Netscape Navigator and Microsoft Explorer are two very popular graphi browsers. They are easy to understand, and only one or two class periods ar required to teach students their essential elements. In order to learn the features of the browser, students should be given access to specific site addresses. Although different browsers offer different features, the basic elements are the same.

The following lesson plans can be used to teach students the basic elements of a Web browser.

LESSON PLAN 1. The following tasks can be done large group style in a class or assigned as a module that students can complete at their own pace.

- Internet Address — Explain the format and use of Internet addresses These addresses are known as URLs, which stands for Uniform Resource Locators. All sites are found using an address that expresse a file path such as, http://www.whitehouse.gov/, in which the *http://* tells the computer to find a hypertext resource at a server located on the WWW (World Wide Web) called *whitehouse.gov*. In a URL, the phrase http stands for Hypertext Transport Protocol. Hypertext contains text or graphics that are "hot links," and selecting those hot links takes one to a different location either in a different document or in the same document. The last part of the previous URL example is *gov*. This indicates a U.S. Government site. The Internet uses a common domain naming system that identifies different types of organizations, computer systems, and individuals. The following list gives domain examples:

    - com — Commercial sites in the United States

    - edu — Educational sites in the United States

    - gov — United States government sites

    - net — Network administrative organizations

    - org — United States organizations

Before instructing students, the teacher should have Web addresses ready for the students to access. The teacher should be sure to visit each site prior to the lesson in order to ensure the site is accessible and appropriate. If firewall software is utilized, many sites may not be accessible and receiving error messages will only frustrate students. Be sure to add all sites to a security system to prevent students from being kept out. Have students key in the URLs. Do not depend on search engines in order to find a site; search engines will be utilized in the second lesson.

- Bookmarks — Have students bookmark the site after the URL is accessed in order that they understand how bookmarks save time when accessing sites in the future. Categorizing bookmarks by topic can be taught at a later time.

- Hypertext — Most sites use hypertext; it is important that students access a site with hypertext in order that the teacher may discuss how hyperlinks are made. Hypertext appears on the Web page in a different color, usually blue. When clicking on this text, a hyperlink is made which accesses another site on the Internet. Hyperlinks allow the user to access related sites without having to type in the URL in a Web browser. Use one example of a link to another location at the same site or in the same document. Show another example in which the link takes the student to an entirely different URL.

- Back/Forward — Once hyperlinks are made, the Back and Forward commands may be utilized by students. The Back and Forward commands are usually located on a button bar in the browser. Each click on the Back command will take students to a previously visited location during the current Internet session. After utilizing the Back command, the Forward command will return students to the site accessed last.

Continue to access sites in order to provide variety, as well as to allow students time to become familiar with browser commands. Once students have accessed a number of sites, allow them to save and print information from those sites. This is important since research papers will be completed using this information.

LESSON 2. The second lesson will instruct students on the use of search engines. The default address on most Web browsers is set to a search engine since students will be utilizing them often. Different search engines give different results so it is important that all students access the same one to begin with. Searches should be demonstrated by the instructor first in order for students to see the results. A scan converter that transfers information from a desktop computer to a television monitor, an LCD panel on an overhead, or a computer projector can be used to show the results of a search to the entire class.

- Choose a topic. The instructor should select a topic for the search. For example, a recent student's research topic was the Ebola Virus.

- Make a list of keywords. Prepare a list of keywords to be used in the topic search using students' input. Discuss which keywords will produce broad results and which will produce more specific results. A few keywords that can be used for research on the Ebola Virus include Ebola, Virus, Health, and Disease. These words can be used individually or in combinations.

- Enter the keywords. Note the number of hits as various keywords are typed into the search engine. Remember, it is possible for broad terms to have fewer hits than specific terms. Continue using keywords and discuss what the students find with each search. For example, using the Alta Vista search engine, the broad keyword, "disease" returned approximately 500,000 hits (related sites). The specific term, "Ebola" used by itself returned approximately 8,000 hits. The term "Ebola Virus" returned over 9,000 hits.

- After the students have used the examples, have them develop keywords for a topic. List five to ten topics for them to choose from and have them develop a list of appropriate keywords. List the keywords found by each student on the board for each topic. These keywords may be examined and compared with other students who searched the same topic.

- As the students progress in their searches, introduce the use of Boolean expressions (AND, OR). For example, students could search for business AND ethics. It is important to note which symbol is used to (1) include all, or (2) to include any. Some search engines require plus (+) signs instead of AND/OR. Although utilizing a variety of search engines (Lycos, Alta Vista, etc.) will enhance any search, it is important to be familiar with the aspects of the particular search engines used in this course.

Each search engine comes with different search basics and uses of the Boolean syntax. They also differ in terms of usage of case sensitive searches. Help menus are available on most search engines. In the first course in which the Internet is introduced, experience suggests that students use only one or two different search engines.

Research Papers

As the business and English departments integrate the teaching of term papers, each department should be responsible for certain elements. The English department should be responsible for topics, preliminary research, conventions, and content. The business department should be responsible for physical format, punctuation, spelling, and research involving the Internet. The English department should initiate instruction on the proper method of documentation and locating of sources for endnotes, footnotes, and other references. It is important for both departments to emphasize checking the accuracy of research found on the Internet.

The Internet contains a wealth of information, but unlike information und in books, magazines, and newspapers, Internet information is not gulated for accuracy. "Since the information found on the Internet repre-ents a unique blend of commercial, educational, governmental, and personal terests, the information you will find cannot be assumed to be authoritative" tegall 1996). To approach the problem of validity of information on the ternet, students should first be informed that research should not begin on e Internet, unless it primarily concerns the Internet. All preliminary re-earch should begin with traditional sources that are critically evaluated. udents can then supplement their research with information from the ternet. By beginning with traditional sources, students also will have a etter eye for what is valid or invalid.

123

valuation of Sites

After finding information on the Internet, students will need guidance in etermining its validity. To determine validity, students should answer the llowing questions:

- Is there an author listed?
- Is the information consistent with other sources?
- Is an e-mail address listed?
- Where is the home page located? For example, is it a college/university site, a government site, or a personal home page?

Since access to the Internet is common and the creation of personal Veb pages is simple, a lot of information may not be valid when using the ternet for research. Anyone with a connection to an Internet server can ace information on the Internet; therefore, students must realize everything n the Internet is not necessarily accurate.

lagiarism

The topic of plagiarism should be covered by both departments. With e advent of computerized information being so readily available, the ease vith which information can be plagiarized increases. Information can simply e cut from an Internet site and pasted to a word processing document. In lassrooms, students should be required to print information to be used in eir papers rather than cut information from the Internet and paste it into eir word processing documents.

ocumentation

Most documentation methods are expanding to accommodate infor-nation found using a variety of sources including the Internet. The 1995 1LA's (Modern Language Association) Guide shows documentation methods f citing e-mail and online sources. The APA (American Psychological ssociation) Style Manual also gives an example of a citation from the ternet.

Information from the Internet can be broken down into separate source such as WWW (World Wide Web), listservs, and e-mail. An example of citing various sources should be given to the students. A common example of a reference citation is given below with permission from Janice R. Walker, University of South Florida at http://www.cas.usf.edu/english/walker/ janice.html:

124

> Author's Last Name, First Name. "Title of Work." *Title of Complete Work.* [protocol and address] [path] (date of message or visit).

Most student research found on the Internet at this level will primarily come from the WWW, Gopher sites, and occasionally e-mail. Examples of these specific sources are presented below. More examples can be found at http://www.cas.usf.edu/english/walker/mla.html.

WORLD WIDE WEB SITES

Burka, Lauren P. "A Hypertext History of Multi-User Dimensions." MUD History. http://www.ccs.neu.edu/home/lpb/mud-history.html (5 Dec. 1994).

GOPHER SITES

Quittner, Joshua. "Far Out: Welcome to Their World Built of MUD." Published in Newsday, 7 Nov. 1993. gopher /University of Koeln/ About MUDs, MOOs and MUSEs in Education/Selected Papers/ newsday (5 Dec. 1994).

E-MAIL

Thomson, Barry. "Virtual Reality." Personal e-mail (25 Jan. 1995).

Research

Students should be encouraged to use traditional means of research to begin looking for topic material. By beginning with traditional sources, students are better prepared to search for information via the Internet. The Internet does not have a specific index to the massive amount of data available on the millions of servers and this makes finding specific information difficult. Students who just "surf" for information are not utilizing the Internet to its fullest potential. The following topics are covered in the document processing course in order to help students find applicable and reliable information on the Internet.

GOPHER SERVERS. Gopher was developed at the University of Minnesota and is a menu-driven application that allows one to look for information. Gopher menus allow one to look through information just as one would search through files and folders in an application such as Windows Explorer. World Wide Web sites are quickly taking the place of Gopher sites since they offer multimedia as opposed to the text-based system of the Gopher. For an example of a Gopher menu, type the following address in a browser's URL location line: gopher://gopher.tc.umn.edu/.

VIRTUAL LIBRARIES. A virtual library holds information in the form of text, pictures, links to related sites, as well as sound and video clips. The information found in a virtual library varies from site to site. An example of a virtual library can be found at the following address: http://acwww.bloomu.edu/ ~ acct/beit.html.

The previous site is the Virtual Accounting Library found at Bloomsburg University and lists links to various sites concerning the topic of accounting.

ERIC. Educational Resources Information Center. This site links to the ERIC database which holds millions of pieces of research material on educational and related topics. The AskERIC site can be found at: http://ericir.syr.edu/.

ONLINE RESEARCH. Many avenues to research on the Internet can be obtained through a fee. Libraries may subscribe to an online service such as Britannica online. For a subscription fee, students can download information found on the Britannica site. The site found at http://www.eb.com/ offers a free trial so that one can see if the service meets the user's needs. Another online research service that charges a fee is the CARL Uncover service found at http://www.carl.org/uncover/. This service is an online periodical and delivery service that charges for articles that are sent by mail or fax.

Using the Internet as a research tool is an excellent way to apply Internet usage in the classroom. It is important to show the educational value the Internet has to offer since it will continue to be a tool available for student use. As more people use the Internet, the number of sites containing relevant and valuable information will increase.

Computer Applications I

A computer applications course is a 10th grade level course for students who have completed Document Processing I. The focus of Computer Applications I is to introduce computer applications including spreadsheet, database, and programming. Internet instruction is continued from Document Processing I with an emphasis on Web page creation. At this point, students have experience accessing information on the Internet and can begin the process of placing information on the Internet. This course provides a better understanding of just how easily information is placed on the Internet and also portrays how the Internet continues to grow.

Placing information on the Internet is not difficult once someone has contracted space on an Internet server. There are many avenues to finding places to hold a Web page. Local Internet carriers charge according to the amount of space used. Many carriers give reduced rates to educational institutions and, in many cases, servers can be found providing free sites.

Internet carriers provide an address, a user ID or (login), and a password. The Internet address will be the URL for the site. A login and password are needed to place information on the Internet via File Transfer Protocol (FTP). FTP is a method for transferring the files between the Web page carrier and the creator of the information. Internet carriers generally require a setup fee for an allotted amount of disk space such as 5MB (megabytes). Additional usage is generally billed at a certain rate per MB each month.

Hypertext Markup Language (HTML) is the language used to create Web pages. HTML is a text-based language that uses "tags" to format elements of the document. An example of an HTML tag is shown below.

< TITLE > Hillsboro Home Page < /TITLE >

The need to know a great amount of HTML code is decreasing as more and more software companies are creating user-friendly applications to build Web pages. These applications include such programs as Hot Dog Pro and Adobe PageMill. Commands are similar to those used to create a word processing program. The Netscape Navigator Gold browser, as well as other browsers, has an editor feature which can be used to teach the process of building Web pages.

The designing and building of a Web page is kept very basic at the introductory computer applications level. The goal is to show students the process of (1) creating a Web page, and (2) how to place it on the Internet. The pages created are generally limited in detail using a combination of backgrounds, text, pictures, graphics, and hypertext. The following basic elements of a Web page should be covered:

- How to apply selected backgrounds to a Web page.
- How to use different font sizes in the creation of a Web document.
- How to place graphics on a Web document.
- How to create hypertext links.

To begin to teach students the elements of a Web page, a Web page is saved from the Internet and loaded into a Web building application such as Adobe PageMill, Hot Dog Pro, or Netscape Navigator's Web editor. Generally any page can be saved, but it is important to find a page that contains all the elements that will be created in the course. Many pages include detailed graphics and animated GIF (graphic image file) images that will not be created in this introductory course. Experience suggests that the teacher create a document to be placed on the Internet containing examples of what is to be utilized in the course. This not only saves time lost searching for an appropriate page, but also gives the teacher the necessary experience creating a Web document and downloading it to an Internet server.

One of the first aspects of an HTML document students will notice is the limitation it has compared to a word processing or desktop publishing application. There are limitations on font sizes as well as the placing of graphics. As students create Web pages, the desire to apply advanced graphics and links will increase. The ability to create more advanced Web pages depends on the multimedia ability of the computer and the software available. Programs such as Adobe Photoshop are valuable when creating images to be placed on the page. Other programs that create animated graphics can be located on the Internet.

If a graphics program such as Adobe Photoshop or Micrografx Picture Publisher is not available to create graphics to be added to Web pages, many

126

images can be found on the Internet. Many of the images found on Internet sites are protected by copyright law, but there are sites available that hold images including pictures, text images, and backgrounds which can be downloaded. One can search the Internet for such images.

Web page projects can provide the opportunity for students to use imagination and creativity. The following project is used after introducing the basic elements of a Web page to assess student learning. It also gives those students with more computer experience the opportunity to use advanced features if proper hardware and software are available.

HOME PAGE PROJECT. Students are assigned the task of creating a section of a school Web page. Depending on course enrollment, two or three students work together to create a section of the home page. The page is designed to give information about the school including academics, athletics, clubs, and other organizations. Even a small school has many areas that could be included in the project. Searching the Internet will provide many school home page sites that can be used as examples. The following criteria are suggested for each group's page.

- Create or select an appropriate background.
- A hypertext link connecting to the main page must be included.
- At least two font sizes are to be used.
- At least two images are to be placed on the page.

The criteria are very basic, yet students are encouraged to be creative and add all elements they think are appropriate to their section. Once the sections are examined by the teacher, they can be added to a folder in order to be placed on the Internet server. Once the initial site is created, future classes can add or update pages.

Many times the graphics and backgrounds students create or import take a large amount of space. These detailed backgrounds and graphics will increase the time needed to load the graphics on many computers. Detailed graphics should be saved with 16 colors rather than 256 colors in order to decrease the file's size.

After students complete their introductory courses, they can obtain further Internet training in more advanced classes such as advanced computer applications, computer programming, and multimedia courses.

References

Stegall, N. L. (1996, December 16). *Using Cybersources.* [Online]. Available: http://www.devry-phx.edu/lrnresrc/ dowsc/integrty.htm.

Walker, J. R. (1996, December 16). *MLA-Style Citations of Electronic Sources.* [Online]. Available: http://www.cas.usf.edu/ english/walker/mla.html.

part III
Internet-Related
Visions and Topics

Chapter 12 — The Cyberprofessional
Association

by Bridget O'Connor
New York University — New York, New York
and
Michael Bronner
New York University — New York, New York

In 1980, the National Business Education Association (NBEA) had approximately 17,000 members; today, it has 12,000; Delta Pi Epsilon (DPE) had about 9,000 members and today it has 4,000. In 1980, the American Vocational Association (AVA) had 50,000 members; today, it has about 36,000. A number of reasons exist for declining participation in professional associations and many of them are financial. However, another reason may be the (mis)perception of the quality of services provided or a feeling that the organization exists for "others — not for me." Professional associations are not volunteer organizations. In a professional organization, you expect some type of payback from your membership. Most of us join professional associations based on a variety of "what's in it for me" interests, and those who get the most out of such organizational memberships are those who are the most active in its activities.

Therefore, this is not a chapter about the Internet. It is a chapter about how we as participants in professional associations can *use* the Internet and the talents of our fellow members to keep our professional edge. The Internet can keep us informed, and by using it, we can become more of a business education community. Moreover, at the same time that we become a stronger community, we are putting out a welcome mat to those outside our field.

Today, nearly every professional has some access to the Internet. However, we have too little understanding of how professionals use — or might use — Internet resources. One way to predict the future is to map the repertoire of current services offered by professional organizations onto Internet resources. Then, we can try to think outside current boundaries, exploring how our participation in professional organizations might further open the door to making us a business education cybercommunity.

The prefix "cyber" is a Greek derivative that means "to pilot" (Jones, 1995). Our cybercommunity can help guide our professional development. But it is mandatory that profession-based learning services be more useful and user-friendly than they are today. Services need to be user-seductive, meaning the more you use them, the more you want to use them. Moreover, as adult learners, active learning or participation is key to personal mastery. In a discussion of how we can participate, we cannot overlook our personality or zest for learning that ultimately controls the amount and kind of our participation. Put another way by T. James Crawford, business education professor emeritus at Indiana University (1980), "No teaching method works unless the learner does." What Internet resources can a professional association tap to seduce its membership and pilot its services?

In this chapter, we will discuss the potential of a variety of Internet resources that support membership needs by matching them to specific services that professional associations offer. The chapter will conclude with Web site addresses (current at the time of this writing) for a number of professional associations related to business education, general education, and our content area specialties.

Conceptualizing the Cyberprofessional Association

Figure 1, Professional Associations' Wheel of Services, conceptualizes the capability of the Internet to support the myriad of services that professional associations offer. The inner circle consists of member services; the outer circle consists of corresponding Internet resources. While the wheel cannot be exhaustive, it is useful here to help visualize the professional association as a hub that links services with useful technological resources. In any given professional association, not

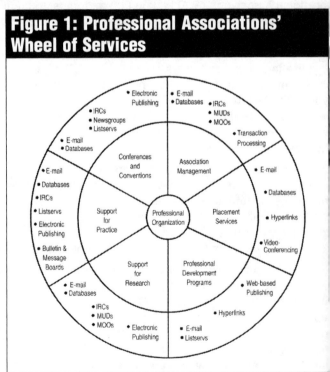

Figure 1: Professional Associations' Wheel of Services

all services may be offered or all technologies used. However, the attempt here is to be as inclusive as possible, suggesting how they map onto six often overlapping services offered by professional organizations.

CONFERENCES AND CONVENTIONS. A major reason most of us belong to professional associations is to learn — to remain current in our field. Many of us attend national or regional conferences to learn more about the best practices and current trends impacting our interests. The major reason many of us go to these conferences is to network. We often learn as much — or more — from "corridor chats" than from formal presentations. Face-to-face contact with our colleagues from other institutions and other regions makes us feel a part of something bigger than our own institution. Getting — as well as giving — support and advice helps refresh and invigorate us.

131

While the Internet cannot substitute for face-to-face encounters, it can substantially augment them. Rather than gaining access to conference proceedings *after* the conference, conference proceedings could be generated *prior* to the meeting for access by members and interested parties. Additionally, conference participants' e-mail addresses could be printed in a preliminary program to allow scholars and practitioners to communicate prior to the meeting about topics or positions.

Conferences and/or conventions are usually held annually; however, most of us need support and advice year-round. When the colleagues we esteem most are actively using Internet resources including newsgroups, listservs, and Internet Relay Chats (IRCs), we can get through those dry spells between conferences and plan ways to make our face-to-face encounters even richer. In addition, being online could also be extended to conference, hotel, food service, and session registration, as well as provide support for ancillary activities sponsored by the host conference committees. The list of possibilities is endless.

SUPPORT FOR PRACTICE. A professional association serves as historian for the profession or discipline that it supports. An understanding of the past aids us in preparing for the future. To this end, the association is a warehouse of useful information. Our colleagues, additionally, can give us feedback as to our own performance. How can we know that what we are doing is right? Are there benchmark practices upon which we can gauge our own performance? As professionals, we business educators are sometimes solely responsible for a given content area/practice in our institution. Even when we are part of an institutional team, we can become insular and unable to examine ourselves critically. Here are some ways we can generate ideas and give, and get, feedback:

- General chat and message boards
- Interactive "Ask the Experts" columns
- Discussion forums on student motivation issues
- Discussion forums on teacher motivation issues
- Bulletin board ideas and graphics

- Three hundred and sixty degree images of effective classroom designs
- Fifty years of statistics related to teaching methods and student achievement

We could also download "Key moments from the profession's history chosen by the current NBEA Board," or "Biographies of inductees into the Business Education Hall of Fame."

Professional organizations can be (soft)warehouses of current and effective ideas for teaching and research practice. Going a step further in technology sophistication, a video gallery of master teachers in action could support effective and innovative instructional methods. NBEA's National Standards and OSRA's Model Curriculum for Organizational and End-User Information Systems, updated regularly, could be linked to key individuals or publishers who provide supporting materials. Conference keynote addresses and full-motion videos of major speakers could also be placed online, going far beyond speaker audiotapes currently provided by many professional associations.

SUPPORT FOR RESEARCH. The Internet has the potential to reconfigure the academic world. Access to publications and their manuscript guidelines can be made easier and disseminated more quickly through sophisticated databases, which already exist. Information can be shared rapidly in both real time and different time modes, reducing the traditional lag time between the initial results of research, its peer review, and its eventual dissemination.

Professional associations often provide support for research projects, such as expert juries or panels who review proposals, and information regarding funding possibilities. Associations provide outlets for research dissemination through their journals, monographs, newsletters, and yearbooks. Many also provide research funds and grants and encourage members to conduct needed surveys. Locating appropriate grant opportunities, obtaining applications, writing the grant, submitting it for peer review, and disseminating results can all be done electronically.

A listserv is an example of different-time information sharing where one user can send information to others' mailboxes easily. Internet Relay Chats (IRCs), Multiple-User Dimension databases (MUDs), and Multiple Object Oriented databases (MOOs), on the other hand, enable not only the sharing of information, they also facilitate the creation of scholarship. IRC is a specific piece of software that uses a common protocol, and IRC has been called the "CB radio of the 90s" (Now What, *Keying In*, September 1996). A more easily accessed version of an IRC is a Multiple-User Dimension (MUD) database that allows multiple users to login via telnet for real-time chats. An extension of MUD is a Multiple Object Oriented (MOO) database, where users manipulate virtual objects, moving from room to room, all in textual form (Day, Crump, Rickly, 1996). Researchers could use MOO:

> ...*To provide divided spaces or channels (the rooms) in which they can work uninterrupted by others, and to allow them to create text-objects,*

such as working drafts or notes, which they can show to other partici-
pants. Just as you might hand around copies of a handout in a
conference room, or project it on the wall, so you share prewritten
texts with others in the MOO. With everyone viewing the same piece
of writing, you can then discuss it and modify it. Each person can
mail the text to him/herself and have an electronic copy at home, or
print it out, revise it, take ideas from it, and then use it to create a
more formal written document, such as one to be published or
presented at a conference (Harrison, 1991).

`133`

Thus, electronic journals could provide a forum not only for the "publica-
ion" of research but also for discussion of ideas posited. This means that
cholars would move from a discrete mode to a continual analysis of opinions.
uch forums, however, must reflect best practices of the field and be main-
ained on a consistent basis to reflect the field's culture.

The communications capabilities of the Internet are just beginning to be
apped as a means to facilitate data collection. For secondary data, public
ccess databases are — and have been — widely available in usable formats.
n example of support for survey data collection is the Public Opinion Poll
istserv where results of survey research — and questions and general com-
nentary — are noted around the world on nearly an hourly basis. A demon-
tration of how quickly data can be collected was offered at the 1996 DPE
Jational Research Conference in Indianapolis, where session leaders Robert
1atyska, Jr. and Nancy Zeliff demonstrated the degree of immediacy of the
levelopment of an online research questionnaire, the gathering of actual data,
he analysis of these data, and a final report — all within a one hour presenta-
ion.

PROFESSIONAL DEVELOPMENT PROGRAMS. One of the most
lifficult — yet ongoing — activities with which we contend is our own
rofessional development. Keeping current with dramatic changes in the
eld; maintaining an effective series of networks with our colleagues and
rofessional associates; and staying abreast of research findings that tend to
verflow in our to-read pile can be overwhelming at best and debilitating at
orst. The Internet can alleviate, if not eliminate, some of these barriers that
re related to access, timeliness, and usefulness.

Associations may develop and/or distribute specifically targeted profes-
ional development programs that might include teaching skills, assessment
nethods, and evaluation techniques. Professional organizations could be
esponsible for the program development process (sponsor and create
rograms); a screening process (identify excellent programs that fit members'
eeds); or part of a certification process (providing evidence of successful
ompletion of learning experiences).

One of the benefits to Web-based learning is that travel time and
xpenses can be eliminated; courses can be offered at "any time/any place"
ccording to the needs of the association's members; and tuition costs — if
nvolved — charged to the member's credit card or association account. This

"just-in-time-training/education" method may enhance greater professional development of the association's members than ever before, and it is possible that a new generation of professionals may find their learning skills sharper than during their college years. The more interactive the learning experiences are, the better the learning experiences.

134

Web-based learning offers many possibilities. A virtual reality leadership experience, for example, could provide innovative examples of interactive "what if" cases involving a wide variety of leadership issues and problems. Not unlike the in-basket projects of old or the newer Looking Glass simulations where one is exposed to a myriad of problems, each demanding prioritizing and action, a virtual reality simulation would pose problems and show real time examples of outcomes resulting from any number of actions. Leadership development fostered in this way could not only enhance individual creativity but also foster greater initiative in individuals involved.

Professional associations are also a primary organizing vehicle for promoting our profession. Professional associations operate as the organizing point for ensuring that our voices are heard by state and national bodies that draft laws and legislation. The Internet was the rallying forum for the American Airlines Pilots' Organization in a decision to strike in 1997. Consider the contributions that business education-related professional organizations could make on issues ranging from School to Work, to Economic Literacy, to Technology in the Classroom.

PLACEMENT SERVICES. The Internet can provide an essential key to job placement for both the organization in need and the individual desiring placement. At the present time, the professional organization publicizes employment opportunities and compiles applicants' placement folders. The applicant and prospective employer meet face-to-face at the conference. This is a time-consuming and costly process to say the least. While face-to-face contact is necessary, a database of positions and an online placement file that can be maintained and updated continually, could augment face-to-face interviews. Furthermore, databases can provide searching options for an applicant or employee, such as content specialty, research interests, and geographic preferences. An applicant's print-based, or any media-based portfolio can be hyperlinked for perusal and downloaded at the leisure of the reviewer. Letters (or voice testimonials) of reference could also be linked. The association's role in this process might be of ensuring the integrity of materials and offering suggestions to applicants and employers alike.

ASSOCIATION MANAGEMENT. For decades, some experts have predicted that network data traffic will exceed voice traffic. Any type of association business — from dues payments to journal subscriptions to applications for association-sponsored life insurance — could be conducted electronically. Journals could be online, membership surveys could be conducted, and even member diversions such as crossword puzzles and games could be offered. In addition, cyberspace membership could make organizations more purely democratic by allowing members to vote on constitutional and by-law revisions, elect officers, and easily use a forum-like approach to examine emerging issues and points of view.

Additionally, in opening up doors to other associations, hyperlinks allow individuals to move from one association's Web page to other related professional development groups or individuals. NBEA linked to OSRA linked to ACM linked to ASTD could allow a dramatic ripple effect of networking that would cross disciplines, organizations, and international boundaries.

135

Summary

This chapter's driving question has been: "What Internet resources can a professional organization tap to attract its membership and pilot its services?"

By definition, a cyberprofessional association is a community of active learners. Active learning implies participation. One way to judge the services that professional associations offer is to gauge how much they are used. As members, we are looking for value-added services from our professional associations. Many Internet resources, such as e-mail directories, listservs, IRCs, MOOs, MUDs, and electronic publishing support a variety of our professional needs. However, changing the way that we communicate with each other, conceptualize a conference, conduct research, and learn new skills requires learning on the part of members as well as the professional organization. As a group, we will change our behaviors only when a majority of our peers do; we will try new communications strategies only when we see them being used effectively and only when we have had an opportunity to experiment with them ourselves. However, our learning curve may be steep (fast!) as the Internet is quickly becoming a vital part of many aspects of our lives. We will be drawn to those professional organizations that provide the most appropriate forums for our learning and sharing.

A caution, however, is to keep in mind that all Internet-based activities demand additional work on the part of *somebody* in the association, and this work can be considerable. A listserv manager, a Web page developer/maintainer, a database entry individual, and/or the Internet provider all demand huge amounts of time and energy, not to mention costs, involved with this process. The effective needs assessment, development, delivery, and evaluation of all types of electronic support systems requires a commitment from the association not only in person hours but in dollars as well. If the membership is to be served in this manner, and served well, it will require additional funds in the form of assessments, additional dues, or other outside sources of revenue. It is true that you "get what you pay for and you pay for what you get." However, if professional development is critical to our field — and we certainly believe it is — then the efforts should be worth their costs.

Again, it is not sharing in the sense of the *transmission* of information that binds a community in cyberspace. It is the *sharing* of information that pulls a community together. The Internet offers us an opportunity to learn and share our ideas in ways that we have not yet envisioned (see Table 1 for a list of various electronic support sites). An association's very existence may depend upon how well it matches the needs of its membership to continually evolving communications tools. The members' "what's in it for me?" is the critical question a successful cyberprofessional organization must address.

Table 1: Electronic Support Sites

- Business Education
  - National Business Education Association — http://www.nbea.org/nbea.html
  - Delta Pi Epsilon (DPE) — http://www.users.intellinet.com:80/~dpe
  - American Vocational Association (AVA) — http://www.avaonline.org
  - American Association of Collegiate Schools of Business (AACSB) — http://www.aacsb.edu

- General Education
  - American Educational Research Association (AERA) — http://tikkun.ed.asu.edu/aera/home.html
  - American Society for Curriculum Development (ASCD) — http://www.ascd.org/index.html
  - Phi Delta Kappa (PDK) — http://www.pdkintl.org

- Training and Human Resource Development
  - American Society for Training and Development (ASTD) — http://www.astd.org
  - Association for Human Resource Development (AHRD) — http://www.ahrd.org
  - Society for Human Resource Management (SHRM) — http://www.shrm.org
  - Training and Development — http://www.tcm.com/trdev
  - *Inside Technology Training* — http://www.ittrain.com
  - *Journal of Technology Education* — http://borg.lib.vt.edu/ejournals/JTE/jte.html
  - *Syllabus* Web — http://www.syllabus.com

- Accounting
  - American Accounting Association (AAA) — http://www.rutgers.edu/Accounting/raw/aaa/aaa.htm
  - Institute of Management Accountants (IMA) — http://www.rutgers.edu/Accounting/raw/ima/ima.htm
  - International Federation of Accountants (IFAC) — http://www.ifac.org

- Marketing
  - American Marketing Association (AMA) — http://www.ama.org

- Finance
  - International Journal of Intelligent Systems in Accounting, Finance, and Management — http://www.bus.orst.edu/faculty/brownc/isafm/isafhome.htm

- Business Law
  - Federal Communications Law Journal — http://www.law.indiana.edu/Vfclj/fclj.html
  - The Journal of Online Law — http://warthog.cc.wm.edu/law/publications/jol
  - The Journal of Information, Law, and Technology — http://elj.warwick.ac.uk/elj/jilt

- Economics
  - AACE International (the Association for Total Cost Management) — http://www.aacei.org
- Information Systems
  - Association for Information Technology Professionals (AITP) [formerly DPMA] — http://www.aitp.org

  - Association for Computing Machinery (ACM) — http://www.acm.org/cacm
  - *Communications of the ACM* — http://www.acm.org/cacm
  - Global Information Systems Education — http://gise.org
  - Office Systems Research Association (OSRA) — http://Walden.MVP.Net/~osra
  - *PlugIn Datamation: The Internet Manager for IS Managers* — http://www.datamation.com
  - *Change Technology* — http://contract.kent.edu/change
  - *T.H.E. Journal* — http://www.thejournal.com
- Office Management
  - Professional Secretaries International — http://www.gvi.net/psi.org
- International Business
  - Global Business Network — http://www.gbn.org
- Higher Education
  - *Chronicle of Higher Education* — http://chronicle.com
  - American Association of University Women (AAUW) — http://www.aauw.org
  - American Association of University Professors (AAUP) — http://www.igc.apc.org/aaup/[due to change]

References

Crawford, J. T. Lecture given at Indiana University, circa 1980.

Day, M., Crump, E., and Rickly, R. (1996). Creating a Virtual Academic Community. In Harrison, Theresa, and Stephen, Timothy, *Computer Networking and Scholarly Communication in the Twenty-First Century University*. (1996). New York: State University of New York Press (pp. 293-294).

Harrison, T. et al., (1991). Online Journals: Disciplinary Designs for Electronic Scholarship. *The Public Access Computer Systems Review* 2.1, 26.

Jones, S. (1995). *Cybersociety: Computer-Mediated Communication and Community*. Thousand Oaks: Sage.

National Business Education Association. (1996, September.) The Internet — Getting Caught Up. (Now What?) *Keying In*. 7:1, 4.

Chapter 13 — Using an Intranet in Business Education

by James E. Bartlett, II
Louisiana State University — Baton Rouge, Louisiana

Computer technologies have improved the methods educators use to communicate. The Policies Commission for Business and Economic Education (PCBEE) has stated in *Policy Statement 53, This We Believe About the Role of Business Education in Technology:* "Business Education will need to adapt to continuous advancements in technology; and the discipline's future will be based, in larger part, on the role it assumes in addressing technological changes." The two biggest advancements that have affected how computer technology is utilized in business education are the appearance of the Internet and Local Area Networks (LANs).

The Internet is a network of computer networks, interlinked at various points around the world, which can communicate with each other. A LAN is a group of computers located in a relatively limited area and connected by communication links that allow them to interact with each other. The Internet and LANs were both designed to permit computer users to communicate and share information. The newest phenomenon is integrating Internet technologies with LANs to create what is known as an Intranet. An Intranet is a group of Web sites that are internal and function as a network using Internet protocols. To avoid confusion, it must be understood that the Internet is not an Intranet.

In 1995, *The Wall Street Journal* predicted Intranets would quadruple in 1996 and would almost triple in 1997. Companies have seen the positive results of using the Internet and have applied the concepts to their local networks. These new Intranets that have been created are showing positive results by increasing productivity, saving money, and enhancing the internal operations of companies. Corporate Intranets will be a key component for companies to compete in the 21st Century.

What Is an Intranet?

When functioning, an Intranet uses the client-server concept. The network server is used to share files, share printers, send and receive electronic mail messages, and store programs. The client, which is the local workstation, requests information stored on the server. The server provides the information requested by the client and then performs the specific task the end-user selected. In some cases, it may be hard to determine the client and the server because they can perform both functions. Since the majority of the information is stored on the server, an Intranet administrator only needs to learn how to update once at the server level, rather than several times at the individual desktop level.

The simplest form of an Intranet is created using a LAN server to store Hypertext Markup Language (HTML) documents and a client computer using a Web browser to view the documents. HTML is the language used to create Web pages. Web browsers interpret this language, then display the Web page to the end-user. This type of Intranet will provide the user with a Uniform Resource Locator (URL) resembling < file://(Server Drive)/directory/index.html > instead of the Internet URL that would resemble < http://www.website.edu/index.html > .

Creating an Intranet

Creating an Intranet can be a rather inexpensive process, if a computer network is currently in existence. All that is needed to create an Intranet is a LAN, Web server, Web browser, and software to create the HTML documents. Web server and Web browser software can be obtained free from the Internet, as can software to create HTML.

There are Web servers for all major operating systems. Some common Web servers are MacHttp and WebStar for Macintosh, WebSever and HTTPD for Windows 3.1, WebSite and Quota NT Server (demo) for Windows 95 and NT. Bear in mind that free software usually does not work as well as its commercial counterpart. However, it is a great way to create an experimental Intranet to sell the idea to an organization hesitant to jump into a larger investment.

Web browser software can be obtained from many different sources for the Macintosh and Microsoft Windows operating systems. If operating in a Microsoft Windows environment, Internet Explorer is distributed free with Windows 95. The Mosaic and Netscape Web browsers can be obtained for both operating systems. All three Web browsers can be downloaded from the Internet. HTML editors can also be downloaded from the Internet. HotDog and HomeSite are both examples of HTML editors. HomeSite is offered free for a limited use trial, and HotDog is available for a free 30-day trial period.

Intranets and National Standards

Educators can use an Intranet for assistance in achieving many of the standards set in the *National Standards for Business Education*. Information

ystems and communications are the two curriculum areas an Intranet would
nquestionably enhance. An Intranet would help introduce students to three
f the five critical areas that should be interwoven throughout all the curricu-
lm areas of business education as defined in *National Standards for Business
ducation*. These three critical areas are communications, human relations,
nd technology.

Using an Intranet, communications standards can be incorporated
nto the curriculum in many different ways. An Intranet will allow stu-
ents and teachers to communicate through sending and receiving elec-
ronic mail messages. While creating HTML documents, students should
e able to master techniques to enhance documents through advanced
ayout, design, and computer graphics production. Advanced students can
earn individually and collaboratively through creating their own Intranets.
students will learn to be proficient in the use of many different software
ackages such as HTML editors, HTML exporters, and graphic enhancers.
When creating HTML documents, students can learn how to operate other
ardware such as digital cameras and scanners to achieve the communica-
ions standards.

The implementation of an Intranet in the classroom would touch upon
hree areas within the recommended information systems curriculum. These
hree areas are: (1) communications systems and networking, (2) common
applications of information systems to organizations, and (3) information
ystems across the curriculum. Students will use, customize, plan, design, and
solve problems using the communications and networking systems, which are
associated primarily with LANs and Internet technologies. When working
with an Intranet, students will be able to maintain and manage the network.
Students will help create parts of the Intranet, while others will be end-users
of the Intranet. The students who are end-users will have access to the
Intranet to obtain information online and navigate to find and share information sources. In many of the situations, students will be using the Intranet to
send and receive electronic mail. When the teachers administrating the
Intranet become comfortable with its use in their classes, the Intranet can be
used across the curriculum in many different classes.

How and Why an Intranet Is Used in Corporations

Since the development of Intranets is in its adolescence, companies are
experimenting with many different uses. Intranets are being used throughout
corporations for electronic publishing, sending and receiving electronic mail,
employee conferencing, filling out electronic forms, searching databases,
completing more complex groupware project management, and aiding in
technical support and help desk. Intranets use the power of Web technologies
and LANs to enhance efficiency within an organization.

Publishing companies using an Intranet are able to publish handbooks,
price lists, and guides at lower costs than traditional publishing methods.
Prior to companies using an Intranet to publish, they had to create the

content, change it to a desktop publishing environment, produce a production draft, make revisions, create a final draft, duplicate the item, and then distribute the publication to the employees. While using an Intranet to publish within a corporation, content can be created, revised, and instantaneously distributed. International Data Corporation completed a study that showed extremely high returns on investment (ROI). On average, the study showed a ROI of 1,000 percent, with a high of 1,800 percent.

Intranets are being used because they decrease cost and complexity of sharing information in an organization. An Intranet can provide a high return on a relatively minimum investment. Any company should be able to build and use an Intranet. Even if individuals are non-programmers, they can build an Intranet and keep it updated. Due to an Intranet operating in a graphical user interface (GUI) environment, users find obtaining and sharing information is not a complex task. This, however, leads to an increase in network traffic. This may be one of the few drawbacks associated with the creation of an Intranet.

Teaching Suggestions

Requiring students to create Web pages using HTML is part of many of the following teaching suggestions. HTML can be created from an HTML editor, HTML exporter, or a simple text editor. HTML editors and exporters can be found on the Internet, while a typical word processing program such as Microsoft Word Pad, Works, Word, or WordPerfect can be used to create a simple ASCII text file using the "save as" command.

SHARING INFORMATION. One of the most common uses of an Intranet is to disseminate information. Using an Intranet to provide information reduces the amount of paper and the cost to share information. In the classroom, educators spend hours copying and handing out papers to students. An Intranet can be used to provide students with their class syllabi, handouts, assignments, references, tutorials, reviews, and tests.

SYLLABI. Using an Intranet, teachers can provide students with an electronic copy of the class syllabus on the network. This enables students to easily access a syllabus and quickly print a hard copy if necessary.

An electronic syllabus on an Intranet can provide students with a schedule of class events, calendars, and assignments. Hyperlinks can be added to allow the page to function as an Internet Web page. For example, students can click on a day on the schedule and see what assignments are due for that class period. In addition to students learning the content aspect of the class, they also learn how to obtain information using a Web browser.

HANDOUTS. Using an Intranet to distribute handouts is an excellent way to provide students with information. This is an immediate benefit of creating an Intranet. Any document that is created on a computer can quickly be transferred to an HTML document. With the use of an HTML exporter, even a PowerPoint presentation can be converted to HTML.

ASSIGNMENTS. Daily assignments can be placed on an Intranet. Assignments can be placed into an HTML document and then viewed by students at the beginning of each class. The use of an Intranet in this manner also combats the problem of missed assignments due to absenteeism. Students can easily go back and view an assignment from the previous day or even week.

REFERENCES. An Intranet can be used to store references and other supplemental materials for students to access. It is possible, and rather easy, to place references on a local Intranet for students. A page that is viewed on the Internet can be saved, modified, and placed on one's local Intranet server. It is important to note that teachers must receive permission from the owner of the page before they do this. Other reference materials can be created by the teacher and placed into an HTML file.

TUTORIALS. An Intranet is a great place to create a tutorial. The Intranet can easily be used in conjunction with other programs. With the ability to multitask, executing two programs simultaneously, students can view a command in the tutorial and then complete the steps in the application.

REVIEWS. With the use of an Intranet, a teacher can create a linear and non-linear review. An interactive quiz game can be created. Students can be asked a question and actively participate by selecting the correct answer. If students click on the correct hyperlink, they will see that their answer was correct, otherwise it will link back and say try again. Reviews can include images, sounds, and videos to increase students' attention. These reviews can be done individually or cooperatively depending on the imagination of the teacher. The teacher's creativity is the only limit to what reviews can do or look like on an Intranet.

TESTS. Testing can even be done over an Intranet. Students could be required to use an Intranet to complete various types of evaluations. Students would view their test or quiz on an Intranet and record their answers on paper or a Scantron-type answer sheet. If the instructor desires, the answers could even be recorded on a file and transferred with electronic mail. This testing procedure could be modified to work for a multiple choice, true-false, essay, or authentic assessment. After correcting students' evaluations, it is possible to mail electronically the results back to them. A copy of the files can be saved if needed.

SCHOOL DISTRICT INFORMATION. Daily school announcements and information can be placed on an Intranet. Students can create HTML documents daily to update school information. A weekly calendar of events might be a place to start and work up to a daily list. This is a great place to put the school sports, plays, and extracurricular activities. Students can look up information or a topic and explore what is available daily.

Student policies and handbooks can also be placed on an Intranet. This service provides a method for students to access information in a timely manner. One policy that should always be available over an Intranet is an

Acceptable Use Policy (AUP). Even though students may not be accessing the Internet from an Intranet, an AUP is still needed.

PROVIDING SOFTWARE AND FILES. Many times in class a teacher wants to provide students with software or files that they might not have. Since an Intranet uses Internet technologies, it is easy to download information from an Intranet. Instructors can place graphics, text files, sounds, and software applications on the Intranet for students to download to the local computer and use. Programs that are shareware or freeware can be placed on an Intranet for students to use and evaluate. By placing files on an Intranet, students learn Internet skills such as downloading, decompressing, and executing files.

144

MARKETING. The Internet has become a marketer's dream. The Internet is a low cost storefront accessible to millions of people. Creating HTML documents allows students to display information on the Internet. Students can use an Intranet that has been created to simulate Internet marketing. Some of the marketing assignments can be fictional, but students can also market real products, school activities, and functions. Students could also integrate marketing with school activities. Students can market sporting events, school shirts, yearbooks, school organization fund raising, and even classes. Each department in the school can have its electronic catalog on the local Intranet.

One interesting concept is to place a school store on the local Intranet. Students can view, purchase, and even advertise items over this system. Students could place orders and then pay for them in the store.

CAREER DEVELOPMENT. Just like the Internet, an Intranet can be used to display electronic resumes. By using HTML, students can create their own interactive resumes. Then, with the use of the school or classroom Intranet, they can display these resumes. Students can use these electronic resumes later on the Internet with slight modifications in the hyperlinks. Throughout the year, students would keep their resumes current. If the students learn another computer skill, they would add the skill to the appropriate section of their resumes. Students could even include a hyperlink to show an example. From this, students will gain an understanding of how Web pages are created and updated.

COOPERATIVE LEARNING. The ability to have students work in cooperative groups is one big advantage of using the Internet, an Intranet, or a LAN. An Intranet is a more controlled network environment than the Internet. This type of environment provides many opportunities for cooperative learning. One example of using an Intranet for cooperative learning is having students complete a reading on Internet topics. To complete this assignment, they must read a specific section and summarize it. Then, after completing this, students post a Web page of their summarized section to the Intranet for the other students in their group to read. Students could make up quizzes on the sections that the teacher can later administer.

STUDENT ORGANIZATIONS. Student organizations can benefit positively from the use of an Intranet. Organizations such as Future Business Leaders of America (FBLA) or Distributive Education Clubs of America (DECA) can have their own Web pages on an Intranet. These pages display club rosters, officers, and even pictures from current organization activities. Club officers and advisors can use the Intranet to place announcements, notices, and important dates. These organizations do not have to be limited to the business department, but someone might want to start with this department so as not to be overwhelmed in the beginning of building an Intranet.

PORTFOLIOS. Electronic portfolios are appearing in many aspects of business and education. Students can create an HTML portfolio by incorporating materials created in business classes, other academic classes, and extracurricular activities. These portfolios will provide a picture of a student and will provide a potential employer information about the student's abilities. Using a digital camera, video camera, and a scanner brings an electronic portfolio to life. Viewing an electronic portfolio with images, videos, and sounds shows a more accurate picture of a person's ability. These portfolios can be modified slightly and placed on the Internet.

CASE STUDIES. An Intranet is a great place to distribute case studies. The Intranet enables students to read the case study and, with the use of electronic mail or a collaborative communications program, discuss the case study. When students have completed the case study, they can respond to the teacher by electronic mail to answer any questions that were asked.

Summary

Educators, students, and administrators need to make use of Intranet technology. Creating and using an Intranet has many benefits for education. A good place to begin is to create a single Web page using HTML, then place it on the server. An Intranet can be a manageable tool. Experience suggests that it is a good idea to start small and proceed with gradual and controlled growth.

Teachers and students should be able to include multimedia functions within an Intranet. Since an Intranet is used over a LAN, the use of audio and video is not as limited as it is on the Internet. Bandwidth is not as much of a concern when operating over a LAN.

Business educators need to adapt with technology to stay abreast in the field of business. Given the speed at which technology evolves, Intranets have an unimaginable potential. The creation of an Intranet in the classroom will be a starting point for students to learn Internet technologies. Students will be able to learn the concepts from an Intranet and apply them to Internet technologies. Intranets will provide business educators an opportunity to enhance students' knowledge and integrate business education throughout other academic classes. See Table 1 for a list of useful resources.

145

Table 1: Resources

- **HTML Creation**
  - Beginner's Guide to HTML — http://www.ncsa.uiuc.edu/General/Internet/WWW/HTMLPrimer.html
  - Background Colors — http://www.infi.net/wwwimages/cell2.html
  - Help for Web Developers — http://www.ondev.com/spmi/web/webbegin.html
  - Intranet and Internet Publishing — http://www.nim.com.au/inet_pub/
  - WebMaster Magazine — http://www.web-master.com

- **Multimedia — Graphics, Sounds, and Animation**
  - The Web Multimedia Tour — http://ftp.digital.com/webmm/fbegin.html
  - Apple's QuickTime VR — http://www.quicktime.apple.com

- **Sample Intranets**
  - Microsoft Office Demo Intranet — http://www.microsoft.com/msoffice/intranet/volcano/tourg001.htm
  - Virtual Intranet — http://www.cplabs.com/dascom/sitepres/sld010.htm
  - Intranet Technology — http://www.stfrancis.edu/ba/ghkickul/ppoint/intranet/index.htm

- **Intranet Resources**
  - Intranet Handbook Page — http://www.ntgi.net/ntg/intra_hb/intra_mm.htm
  - Intranet Development Page — http://www.dsdelft.nl/~intranet/
  - Intranet FAQs — http://www.intrack.com/intranet/faqbasic.shtml

- **HTML Editors and Exports**
  - HotDog Professional — http://www.sausage.com/hotdog32.htm
  - HomeSite — http://www.allaire.com/main.cfm
  - Internet Assistant for PowerPoint — http://www.microsoft.com/powerpoint/internet/ia/
  - Netscape Gold 3.1 — http://www.netscape.com

References

Bremner, L., Iasi, A., and Servati, A. (1997). *Intranet Bible.* Nevada: Jamsa Press.

Crispen, P. (1997). *Atlas for the Information Superhighway.* Cincinnati, OH: South-Western Educational Publishing.

CyberAtlas. (1996). *Intranet.* [Online]. Available: http://www.cyberatlas.com/intranet.html.

Graziadei, W. (1996, November). *The Intranet - Revolution or Evolution?* [Online]. Available: http://137.142.42.95/slides/intranet.html.

Intranets: Internet Technologies Deployed Behind the Firewall for Corporate Productivity. Prepared for the Internet society INET'96 annual meeting. [Online]. Available: http://www.process.com/intranets/wp2.htp.

JSB Computer Ltd. (1995, November). *Intranet- A Corporate Revolution.* [Online]. Available: http://www.intranet.co.uk/papers/intranet/fintranet.html.

Korzeniowski, P. (1997, January). *Intranet Bets Pay Off, Corporations Are Leaping Headfirst Into Intranet Waters, Eschewing Traditional Return on Investment.* [Online], 19, 2. Available: http://www.infoworld.com/cgi-bin/displayArchives.pl?dt_iwe02-97_75.htm.

Miller, M. (1996, March). *Your Own Private Intranet.* [Online]. Available: http://www8.zdnet.com/pcmag/issues/1505/pcm00010.htm.

ational Business Education Association. (1995). *National Standards for Business Education: What America's Students Should Know and Be Able to Do in Business.* Reston, VA: National Business Education Association.

ational Business Education Association. (1996, September). The Internet—Getting Caught Up. *Keying In*, 7, 1.

etscape Communications Corporation. (1996). *Press Clippings.* [Online]. Available: http://home.netscape.com/comprod/at_work/press_clippings/index.html.

olicies Commission for Business and Economic Education. (1959-1996). *This We Believe About the Role of Business Education in Technology, 1993.* Policies Commission for Business and Economic Education Policy Statements. Cincinnati: South-Western Educational Publishing.

rocess Software Corporation. (1996). *Serving Up a Winning Intranet Solution.* [Online]. Available: http://www.process.com/intranets.

way Communications. (1997). *So What Is an Intranet?* [Online]. Available: http://www.rway.com/rway/intranet.htm.

hyfault, M. (1996, January). *The Intranet Rolls in.* [Online]. Available: http://techweb.cmp.com/iw/564/64iuint.htm.

ona Research Incorporated. (1997). *Internet and Intranet: 1996 Markets, Opportunities, and Trends.* (2nd Ed.). [Online]. Available: http://www.zonaresearch.com/reports/inet2.htm.

147

Chapter 14 — Community Networks: Pathways to a Revitalized Society

by Douglas Schuler
Seattle Community Network — Seattle, Washington
Cynthia Denton
Western Montana College of the University of Montana — Dillon, Montana
and
Larry Denton
Hobson High School — Hobson, Montana

Global forces — societal and technological — have shattered traditional communities in a multitude of ways. Citizens may feel as if they have become faceless entities, lost in an undifferentiated crowd. At the same time, they feel isolated and alone, disconnected from any human community. Communities are a natural focus for addressing today's problems. For one thing, many current social problems are community problems — poverty, crime, unemployment, drug abuse, to name only a few. These problems are manifest in the world and are best examined and dealt with by a community, since communities are a familiar and natural unit.

The old concept of community is obsolete in many ways and needs to be updated to meet today's challenges. The old or "traditional" community was often exclusive, inflexible, isolated, unchanging, monolithic, and homogeneous. A new community — one that is fundamentally devoted to democratic problem-solving — needs to be fashioned from the remnants of the old.

A new community is marked by several features that distinguish it from the old community. The most important is that it is *conscious*. In other words, a community will need a high degree of awareness — both of itself and of the culture in which it exists. Further, the consciousness of the new community is both intelligent and creative. The intelligence of a new community comes from its store of information, ideas, and hypotheses; its facility with negotiation, deliberation, and discussion; its knowledge of opportunities and circumstances, as well as its application of technology such as the internet. The creativity of a new community comes from its ability to reassess situations and devise new, imaginative, and sometimes unexpected methods for meeting community challenges.

Business Education

150

Business education can play a vital role in the transition from the "old" community concept to the "new" community concept. Society is constantly changing. Modern transportation systems and communication technology accelerate change, as do other upheavals, both social and environmental. For those reasons, determining concrete business education goals is an uncertain and ambiguous enterprise. How can we educate for the 21st century when we cannot realistically expect to know what it will be like? Our approach to business education must, therefore, be flexible and somewhat open-ended.

Business education is not simply a set of skills — education must also impart an outlook or perspective that prepares individuals for the future. When business education actually helps to address this need, it becomes an active institution for community development. When business education fails in this task, it becomes an impediment, a useless vestige of days gone by.

The broad aim of business education should be to help individuals become more competent, thus indirectly benefiting the larger society. It should also instill a social ethic, allow us to engage in discourse with others, help us to accept and appreciate different viewpoints, and urge us to take action that benefits society and the natural world.

Business education should help produce citizens who are just and prudent, as well as intelligent and effective. Society can adapt to changing times if its citizens are able to help themselves and others, have strongly developed civic and social ethics, and can intelligently and creatively face challenges.

We need to create business education structures to help every individual develop intellectual independence and a sense of empowerment. Its purpose must be to help form active and questioning citizens who can participate fully in society. If business education helps the individual, it helps, by extension, the community, industry, and government.

The widespread availability of electronic networks may create substantial transformations in business education in the near future. However, the need for facilitators of education traditionally called "teachers," educational material ("books"), physical and virtual places where learning is the chief enterprise ("schools"), coordinated events that facilitate learning ("classes"), and courses of studies ("formal education" and "curricula") will remain.

Computer networks offer two basic capabilities to business education. The first is that information can be disseminated over a vast distance and to select or diffuse groups of people quite easily. The second capability offered by this technology is that new forms of collaboration are now possible.

Business education must be integrative. Just as business education must be part of the community, the community must be part of business education. Schuler (1996) points out that one "recent innovation is creating educational institutions in partnership with other community institutions."

The concept of a community of learning is a powerful one that contains at least two important ideas for the development of these new communities. The first is that business education and communities need to be interlinked into one community, where the community helps support business education (e.g. through information, tours, volunteering, and financial support) and the educational system helps the community (e.g. through civic action, job training, and resource sharing). The second idea is that classrooms — virtual or otherwise — need to become communities of learning where students and teachers alike work cooperatively to ensure that everyone's educational experience is as useful and rewarding as it can possibly be.

While virtually every conceivable post-school occupation involves working with other people to achieve some objective, schools, as a whole, are remarkably deficient in the area of cooperative group work. If students do not learn how to work together, they will be deprived of valuable learning experiences, and will not make use of a valuable untapped resource for learning in the classroom — other students. Roger Johnson and David Johnson (1988) define cooperative learning situations as "having positive goal interdependence with individual accountability." In other words, each student must gain mastery or perform at a certain level, but may obtain additional rewards if the group does well. The students do not just work in groups — they work cooperatively in groups toward shared goals.

Johnson and Johnson draw the following four conclusions about cooperative interaction from the data of over 500 studies: (1) Students achieve more; (2) Students are more positive about school, subject areas, and teachers or professors; (3) Students are more positive about each other; and (4) Students are more effective interpersonally. They sum up the indispensable nature of cooperative learning as follows, "Being able to perform technical skills such as reading, speaking, listening, writing, computing, problem solving, etc. are vaulable but of little use if the person cannot apply those skills in cooperative fashion with other people in career, family, and community settings." Business education can be used advantageously in a wide variety of collaborative programs that can benefit the community/business education partnership.

Students need to feel that their education has relevance and value or they will reject it as boring, artificial, and meaningless. Therefore, it is critical that the business education program be useful to individuals, families, and the entire community. When students are actively engaged with problems or issues that concern them, a stronger and deeper respect between teacher and student emerges. Solving problems individually and in groups through planning and acting is also indispensable to business education. Techniques may include hypothesizing and experimenting, tracking down information, interviewing people, understanding issues through dialogue and argumentation, and developing good work habits and discipline. Becoming fluent with a variety of these approaches and knowing when and how to employ them will remain important no matter how much technology may change.

There is no end to the number of problem-solving projects that are educational as well as useful and relevant to the community. Some of these include neighborhood mapping; community histories; interest or opinion surveys; or developing catalogs of information; organizations, services, and other community assets. Many institutions from middle schools to universities are now requiring or otherwise encouraging students to take part in community activities, often through the granting of credits. Business education has the opportunity to drive the movement of school, student, and community collaboration.

Community Networking Centers

As the "new" community unfolds, community networking centers and business education programs can collaborate to provide training for all citizens. The traditional school setting is an essential part of the new evolving community structure. A complementary part of this structure is the community networking center. Obviously, community networking centers can be virtual or physical entities. When the center is an actual, physical location in the community, equipped with computing facilities, it has both social and economic advantages. The center promotes a community orientation and can take the form of empowering individuals.

For educational purposes, the possibility of co-teaching and collaborative project opportunities is much higher when a physical location, as well as a virtual location for such activity, exists. Those who work at the community networking center — whether it be paid staff, student interns, or volunteers — can answer questions or refer more challenging questions to citizens with more expertise. Community networking centers of this type are examples of community empowerment where citizens gain skills and knowledge to become researchers and advocates as well as learners. Business education has always had these goals, and with the evolution toward community networking centers, business educators have an additional tool to reach a larger population.

Community networks (through which free or very low cost access to computing and communication resources is made readily available to the entire community [Schuler, 1996; 1997]) offer an opportunity for revitalizing business education by suggesting modifications of older methods and by providing new methods of conducting business education. Some of the new online educational modes are:

- Virtual study-group or seminar.
- Co-education.
- Hybrid electronic/traditional courses such as homework helping.
- Correspondence or distance learning courses.
- Collaborative "distributed" projects such as the measuring of the earth or (monitoring) weather.
- Educational contracts between teachers and learners.

- Access points at schools and at educational centers in the community.

These modes of education can promote business education in unstructured and structured ways. Providing access to community information and network resources, with no imposed structure, allows people to pursue their own education. More structured approaches involving professional educators, schedules, and guidelines are also possible.

153

Community networks can provide a variety of educational material online, bringing both the library and the educational archive into the home. Community networks also offer conversational capabilities that are more significant than simply providing another way to access static information. The conversational capabilities provide an opportunity for all players in the business educational arena — students, teachers, parents, policymakers, and other community mentors — to enter into conversations regarding business educational policy. They can also consider the rights and responsibilities of each of the players and participate in both the content and process of business education. Community-network systems can play a part in this metamorphosis toward what educational consultant Edward Fiske calls "learning communities" by providing a live forum for the interplay of these new ideas.

The seeds of a democratic educational system do exist today. Many teachers and administrators want to expand the dialogue to involve students, their families, and the rest of the community. At the same time, many students, family, and community members also want to enrich, extend, and breathe new life into existing business educational programs, as well as develop new ones. Clearly, we can go further in the direction of establishing a business education structure that is responsive to people's needs.

Information can help community members in a variety of other ways as well. People who need goods or services or have something to offer may place a want ad in a newspaper, neighborhood message-board, or community computer network. People may need information related to employment, such as job listings, job counseling and training, information on job searches, and information about unemployment benefits and other programs. This information could easily be made available electronically; applying for unemployment assistance or other programs could also be handled electronically. Richard Civille, for example, in his study on "The Internet and the Poor" (1995) believes that civic and community networks could provide valuable job bank services."

Unemployed people may also need training or access to other educational opportunities. They may want or need to meet with other unemployed people to discuss their feelings, job-seeking strategies, or even ideas about starting their own businesses. When there are large layoffs in the community, affected workers, their families, and other people in the community need a forum for discussing these issues or for raising concerns with management of the company doing the layoffs. Workers, whether employed or not, often feel isolated and powerless, and community networks could help provide a new platform for a public voice, organization, and solidarity. Business education programs in collaboration with community networking centers can address these needs.

Community members also need information and support on other economic issues such as how to start small businesses. They need information on available programs, legal requirements and regulations, banking and loans, marketing ideas, model business plans, and alternative organizations like cooperatives. Organizations such as the Better Business Bureau, the Chamber of Commerce, and the Small Business Association all have useful information on these topics, which could become electronically available. Kretzmann's and McKnight's book, *Building Communities From the Inside Out* (1993), contains an invaluable section on "Rebuilding the Community Economy." The Center for Neighborhood Technology (1992) also offers a useful guide on business creation and development. The need for non-traditional learning centers is becoming evident. The business educator and community networking center can create these learning centers which will be of tremendous benefit to all communities.

Lifelong learning has become an essential survival skill. Ongoing learning from the home greatly extends the learning opportunities for young-sters as well as adults. School networking and community networking are merging around the theme of K-100, lifelong learning in an enjoyable context. Since students spend only a fraction of their time in school, the community networking concept opens up much more time for learning. Many students find the self-directed interactive features of telecomputing more motivating than passively watching television. There are successive levels of self-empow-erment: (1) The ability to search the World Wide Web (WWW) for information and teach oneself whatever one would like to know; (2) The ability to create a community of information sharing contacts locally and globally; and (3) The ability to self-publish for both entrepreneurial purposes and to interact with and teach others. Business education is poised and prepared to lead the self-directed, lifelong learning movement.

Online Mentoring

Traditional and non-traditional students need training, which business education provides. With continued technological development and electronic communication, teaching and learning will need to adapt. Self-directed learning using electronic media can be fertile territory for business educators who are willing to become online teachers and mentors. The business educators who assume these needed roles must realize they will be playing three different roles throughout the process. One role of a mentor is that of a local guide. The mentor attempts to smooth the entry of the novice into a new situation, help the novice get to know the ropes, and to provide techniques and tips to survive the beginning online stages. The second role is that of an online companion assisting the novice to shape appropriate techniques and attitudes for online work. The third role of the mentor is that of change agent encouraging novices to integrate online techniques into their curricular and academic work.

The online mentor assists the novice in working with online conferencing. Online environments can enhance three aspects of learning: idea generation, idea linking, and idea structuring. The first is easily realized by the distribution of information using telecommunications, followed by an online discussion, debate, or brainstorming session on a listserv. Idea linking involves identifying associations among ideas and connecting new material to these linkages. Idea structuring involves organizing the ideas and linked concepts into some kind of hierarchical or sequential structure that will allow the ideas to be put into action.

As business education programs adapt to serving expanded populations in a distributed format, it is important that the mentor of an online event be aware of how this process differs from face-to-face situations. Online group learning is student-centered and requires a different role for the teacher. The teacher becomes a mentor or facilitator. The mentor plans the activities but then follows the flow of the conversation, offering guidance as needed rather than strictly adhering to the preplanned agenda or syllabus. Levin (1995) suggested several guidelines for successful online projects with mentors or facilitators:

- **STRUCTURE.** The networked activity needs to occur within a defined structure. The structure might be defined by a set of lessons, or by a sequence of tasks.

- **PROCESS.** The activity is outlined with clearly defined phases. A telecollaborative activity might, for example, have an introductory phase, a data collection phase, and a reporting phase. An online course might be divided into a series of lessons, each of which has an information presentation phase and an activity.

- **MEDIATION.** A key commonality of successful online projects is the role played by an active and effective moderator to initiate and sustain interaction.

- **COMMUNITY-BUILDING.** Successful projects occur within groups that see themselves as part of a close-knit community.

- **INSTITUTIONAL SUPPORT.** The networks and the collaborative activities that they support need to be imbedded within an institutional structure, which provides security and continuity.

Harasim, Hiltz, Teles, and Turoff (1995) identified some of the techniques that have proven most useful for online mentors. They are:

- Create a casual, warm, welcoming, and supportive atmosphere.

- Make participation expectations clear.

- Do not lecture. An elaborate, long, text-based presentation can produce silence.

- Model responsiveness — especially for the first assignments.

- Encourage students to compliment or respond to one another.

- Positively reinforce discussion contributions, and negatively reinforce silence.
- Close a discussion with a synthesis or weaving of the topic.
- Ask participants to tell how they feel about the course.
- Use telephone, fax, or e-mail to make sure that activities are well-coordinated.

156

Through the collaboration of traditional education practices and the electronic media community network center concept, business educators will become leaders in their communities by providing all citizens the opportunity to become productive, working members of the community.

Summary

This chapter has focused on the development of community networks as one way to help anchor and safeguard "new communities." Of course, community networks are meant to be just one aspect of a new society — a society that is more democratic, flexible, inclusive, equitable, and sustainable than the current one.

A community revitalization or "renaissance" — of which community networks are just one part — cannot be carried out by single individuals, nor can it be achieved by a single institution or corporation. It will be necessary for thousands or millions of people and organizations with a strong and urgent sense of social responsibility to join together and push firmly forward toward an equitable and sustainable community. A community must indeed be a web, a series of interlocking elements linking people and places together for a common good and towards a common goal. Business education is poised to play a strong role in this movement, and technology including the Internet will supply important communication resources and services.

References

Civille, R. (1995). The Internet and the Poor. In Kahin and Keller (1995).

Fiske, E. (1991). *Smart Schools, Smart Kids.* New York, NY: Simon and Schuster.

Harasim, L., Hiltz, S. R., Teles, L. and Turoff, M. (1995). *Learning Networks: A Field Guide to Teaching and Learning Online.* Cambridge, MA: The MIT Press.

Johnson, R., and Johnson, D. (1988, Winter). Cooperative learning. *In Context.*

Kretzmann, J., and McKnight, J. (1993). *Building Communities From the Inside Out.* Evanston, IL: Center for Urban Affairs and Policy Research, Northwestern University.

Levin, J. A. (1995). Organizing Educational Networks: Step Towards a Theory of Network-Based Learning Environments. In a paper presented at the 1995 annual American Education Research Association Conference, San Francisco.

Rogan, J. (1996). *Online Mentoring.* Reach for the Sky Project.

Schuler, D. (1996). *New Community Networks: Wired for Change.* Reading, MA: Addison-Wesley Longman Publishing Company. (Excerpts from pages 8, 9, 74, 89, and 103 reprinted by permission of Addison-Wesley Longman.)

Schuler, D. (1997). Community Networking Movement. [Online]. Available: http://www.sch.org/ip/commnet.

Chapter 15 — Beyond the Internet: A Virtual Education Environment

by Hazel R. Walker
Mainline Information Systems — Tallahassee, Florida

Technology has changed the techniques we use to deliver education. This change has become so profound that a new organizational structure has emerged. This new structure is evidenced by education at all levels and all academic disciplines — a virtual education. The terminologies "Virtual College," "Virtual University," and "Virtual High School" permeate our literature and help describe a Virtual Educational Environment at the secondary and postsecondary levels of education.

A second trend, globalization, has advanced to the point in business and in education that an expanded set of management structures leads educational institutions and governing bodies to implement a formal virtual administrative support structure. Globalization and the ability to provide educational services over great distance has pushed forward due to advancements in voice, video, and data systems (Bradley, Hausman, and Nolan, 1993).

Just as in business, educational institutions are able to capitalize on market niches that are too small, too remote, or too expensive to serve by delivering courses in the traditional manner of faculty on-site with a group of students. However, educational institutions can fully service these markets with advancing technology. An institution can now deliver a full range of educational services "virtually" to students at any location on the globe who have access to the supporting technology. In the information systems field, the term "enterprise networking" would be used to indicate that organizational structures can "work together apart" (Grenier and Metes, 1992).

Figure 1 (adapted from *Globalization, Technology, and Competition*) illustrates that the drivers of change are globalization and technology. These drivers have provided the bases for a new competitive environment through a new educational structure. This structure is coined as a "Virtual Education Environment or VEE." The response from boards of regents, trustees, and college university administration is to compete to its markets with the offering of degrees, courses, and knowledge-based learning utilizing powerful networks as the delivery infrastructure. As this figure illustrates, new organizational structures have emerged throughout education.

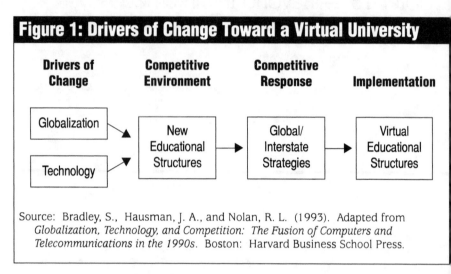

Figure 1: Drivers of Change Toward a Virtual University

Source: Bradley, S., Hausman, J. A., and Nolan, R. L. (1993). Adapted from *Globalization, Technology, and Competition: The Fusion of Computers and Telecommunications in the 1990s.* Boston: Harvard Business School Press.

Educational institutions are clamoring to organize and add a complete administrative infrastructure and delivery model for this Virtual Education Environment. Business education, indeed, has also been affected by this new organizational structure. As managers, support personnel, and instructional personnel, we have all been affected by the infusion of technology into our academic programs — mainly integrating the use of the Internet and computer technology courses into our curricula. We now move "Beyond the Internet" and add the Virtual Educational Environment to our profession.

Virtual Education: A Definition

Pennsylvania State University, one of the United States' foremost leaders of virtual education (also known as distance learning), proffered the following view within a report from its Task Force on Distance Education (The Report of Task Force on Distance Learning, 1992).

- Learner and educator (and/or learner and educational institution physical structures) are geographically remote from one another.
- Students are not present at the time and place when instruction is provided.
- An asynchronous learning environment is present.
- Instruction for students is augmented with communications support.

- Learner engages in communications with educator, other students, institutional personnel, via voice, video, data systems, and networks.
- Formal education processes are provided for course credit, degrees, or knowledge-based learning.
- Learner must acquire knowledge, skills, and attitudes based on the objectives of the course of study.

159

- Learner must gain an understanding of the value and application of the knowledge.

Educational institutions are providing a global, capability-based environment that integrates sound instructional and research methodologies and full administrative processes augmented with powerful, advanced system and network technologies. These trends are now providing education any time, any place, anywhere from accredited institutions and organizations for degrees, courses, and knowledge-based learning — a Virtual University environment. A Virtual Education Environment is defined as offering **all** educational services to remote students with advanced technology.

ILLUSTRATIVE SERVICES FOR A VIRTUAL EDUCATIONAL ENVIRON-MENT. The Virtual Education Environment provides services along four venues:

1. Delivery of education to multiple sites — traditional students
   a. Using content experts, industry lecturers, and "hot topics" to augment courses and lectures.
   b. Downloading information from multiple sources and in multiple data formats into "multimedia" or "multiple media" presentations.
   c. Teaching low enrollment courses at multiple campuses.
   d. Evaluating instruction remotely.
   e. Teaching remediation courses remotely from participation with remediation experts at the high school or community college level.
   f. Conducting research via online access to libraries and the new virtual libraries including access to our nation's prestigious universities, national museums, and corporate libraries.
   g. Supporting student requests with multiple electronic messaging tools with timely responses from faculty and support personnel.

2. Delivery of education to off-campus and/or non-traditional students at the workplace or home
   a. Accredited courses leading to degree
   b. Professional licensure, certification, and/or continuing education units
   c. Adult education enrichment

d. Advanced placement courses

e. Augmentation of home schooling

f. Remediation

g. Extension of campus to disabled students

h. Extension of campus to geographically challenged students

3. Provision of streamlined administrative services

a. Applications: examples

i) Admissions

ii) Housing

iii) Financial aid

b. Electronic Funds Transfer

i) Tuition and fees

ii) Scholarships

iii) Books and materials charges

c. Analysis of Articulation Agreements

d. Analysis of transfer credits

e. Electronic Data Interchange (EDI) to build databases

f. Distribution of test scores, grades, transcripts, forms, and supporting documentation to support administration

g. Audit and accreditation processes

4. Instructional management

a. Assessment and evaluation: real-time instruction, pre- and post-test

b. Student and faculty reporting, grade book administration

c. Communication support systems for 1:1, 1:few, and many:many

d. Faculty development and training

e. Course development support

These four venues can enhance education structure. A shift utilizing these support services is starting to be seen at some K-12 school districts and many postsecondary institutions. Thus, an emerging model for a Virtual Education Environment will probably include the above four service venues.

Paradigm Shift for New University Structures

The Virtual Education Environment is not a "technology fad." Our political leaders are upgrading their institutions with virtual and distance learning options, retrofitting their networks and facilities to support high-speed networks for voice, video, and data systems and information repositories. Adding fiscal resources into the education budgets is part of the standard perating budget of the institution. "The past gives no answers to present-day roblems. The past only has lessons showing us that we can no longer live ke we did" (Gorbachev, 1986).

The Center for Educational Technology at Florida State University eveloped a model of the overall structure of electronic systems. This view Figure 2) forms the basis of an information architecture to support a view of a irtual Education Environment.

161

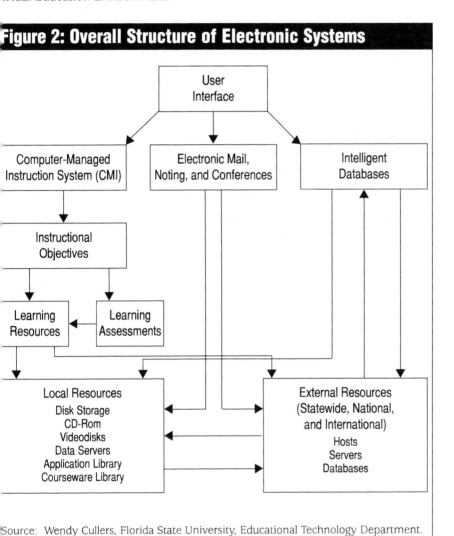

Figure 2: Overall Structure of Electronic Systems

Source: Wendy Cullers, Florida State University, Educational Technology Department.

The Western Governors' Association (WGA), composed of governors rom 13 western states, has organized itself into an educational consortium to eliver postsecondary degrees and programs through a "Virtual University" vith a regional orientation.

As governors, we are concerned about higher education because we know it serves as the gateway to the "good life" for many citizens — helping people acquire the skills, knowledge and abilities to compete in the workforce. At the same time, we are troubled about the ability of higher education to meet increasing demands — keeping educational opportunities of high quality, affordable, accessible, and relevant. A virtual university would be an alternative, break-the-mold approach to higher education, harnessing the latest advances in technology and telecommunications. . . . (Western Governors Report, 1996)

The Western Governors University (suggested name) outlined three steps to develop a virtual university granting degrees to its constituencies:

- **VIRTUAL CATALOG.** Electronic learning opportunities will be organized in an online catalog that will allow students to find courses from both public and private colleges and universities, as well as other providers of instruction and training.

- **DEGREE-GRANTING INSTITUTION.** Not a teaching institution, rather a broker, integrator, and facilitator to help students assemble academically coherent sets of courses from perhaps several institutions to count toward degrees or certifications.

- **NEW GENERATION LEARNING INSTITUTION.** This institution would award degrees or certifications based upon assessment of true competency and learning without regard to where, when, and how that learning was acquired. A market-oriented learning system that facilitates and brokers corporate training as well as traditional academic education.

The Educational Commission of the States, composed of the 50 states' governors, has developed an organization that is providing an online information service to inform the public about current issues in education. These governors meet and review the relevant educational issues including technology and accountability. The impact of virtual education programs through technology upon our schools has great political impact for our leaders. Their findings and recommendations are then posted on the Web. The Web site is http://www.ecs.org.

A requisite reading for political and educational leaders and faculty implementing and planning their Virtual Education Environments is "Learning in the New Millennium: Toward the 'Virtual University'." This article addresses the central core of the university that may be enhanced with a new delivery arm: an online or virtual program. Hutchison discusses the idea of a university, the exponential growth of information, the new technologies, and the movement toward a virtual education (Hutchison, 1996).

Age of Transformation

Virtual Education Environments are also present within the community college systems and its leaders. King, Koller, and Eskow (1997) espouse that this is the "Age of Transformation" for institutions — continual re-engineering, restructuring, and reinventing organizations and institutions — with growing needs for information access and better communications. To be successful, people must remain current in key aspects of technology, commerce, and global activities.

Brevard Community College (BCC) is a member of the Division of Community Colleges of the Florida Department of Education. BCC is recognized as an innovator in its educational philosophy and methodologies to include educational technology to expand its mission. It is located in the nation's space capital and is a public college that provides degrees, certificates, courses (credit and noncredit), professional training, lifelong learning, and community and cultural services. BCC has five campuses that include a virtual campus. The BCC Online Campus is the college's fifth campus. (See Figure 3.)

163

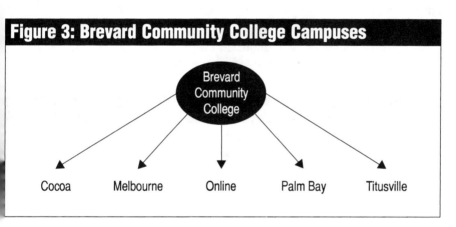

Figure 3: Brevard Community College Campuses

Since the online campus was not built with 'bricks and mortar,' it costs taxpayers nothing to build and operate (physical facilities). Brevard Community College has a support infrastructure for its information networks and servers, as well as an education program for all faculty for the online campus. These costs are included within their annual budget. In addition, it is a non-polluting, energy-saving campus. It has no air conditioners or furnaces, produces no waste, and creates no traffic jams. It was built to free students from the obstacles of space, time, and money.

Dr. Maxwell King is President of the Brevard Community College District. He and his five campus presidents "are proud to make our degree programs, courses, customized corporate training, and student services available to you and the rest of the 20 million people who are online around the world . . . ." This online, virtual fifth campus offers its students all the services of the local campuses — library, learning resources centers, academic advising, financial aid, faculty offices, student union and bookstore, student organizations, student and school publications, discussions, and socializing. BCC provides these services and "places" within the Electronic University Network on America Online.

Dr. Tace Crouse, Cocoa Campus President, was queried as to the most difficult challenge in restructuring BCC to support its Online Campus paradigm. Dr. Crouse indicated that "the education of current faculty with new tools and methodologies was a challenge that they have successfully met" (Telephone Conference with Walker, 1996). Each faculty member receives ongoing professional development for the online campus. Dr. Crouse and her colleagues reiterate that their online campus offers the same quality instruction and services found on all campuses, including the same goals, objectives, skills, and competencies.

Delivery Models/Institutional

Currently, four delivery models emerge from the offerings of virtual education programs as Figure 4 illustrates.

    1. **EXISTING INSTITUTIONS ADDING VIRTUAL EDUCATION PRO-GRAMS.** Many institutions and some school districts have established formal virtual university or distance learning charters. Formal

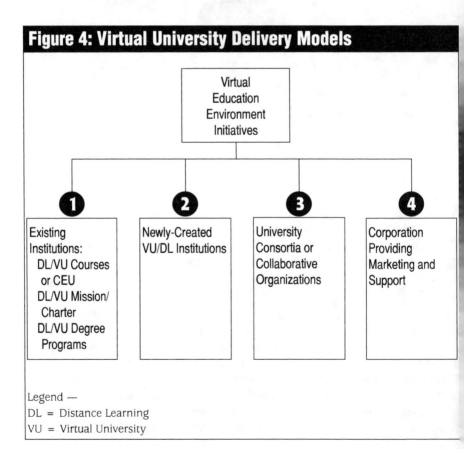

Figure 4: Virtual University Delivery Models

Virtual Education Environment Initiatives

1 Existing Institutions:
DL/VU Courses or CEU
DL/VU Mission/ Charter
DL/VU Degree Programs

2 Newly-Created VU/DL Institutions

3 University Consortia or Collaborative Organizations

4 Corporation Providing Marketing and Support

Legend —
DL = Distance Learning
VU = Virtual University

programs have been developed for the extended mission of the organization. These programs provide accredited courses, degrees, and continuing education programs. They may also provide continuing education credit units, seminars, and industry training via a virtual education model. They provide the administrative and student services through their on-campus and interactive distance learning programs. Additionally, they have developed an administrative structure to support this mode of education from their institutions. Some of the leaders within the United States are:

a. Pennsylvania State University

b. University of Minnesota

c. University of Missouri

d. Florida State University

e. University of Phoenix

f. California: University and State University System

g. Emporia College in New York

2. **NEWLY-CREATED EDUCATIONAL INSTITUTIONS.** A second model is the institution that is *created* to provide education in whole, or part, with virtual or distance learning network options. Illustrative programs are the following:

a. Virtual Online University (VOU).

   i) VOU is an accredited liberal arts institution.

   ii) VOU operates solely on the Internet.

b. Florida Gulf Coast University.

   i) The newest university in the United States chartered to offer its programs both on-campus and through educational technology to remote students.

   ii) Florida Gulf Coast University is located in Fort Myers, Florida.

c. Montgomery College, Woodlands, Texas.

   i) The newest junior college in United States with a distance learning charter and advanced network facilities.

   ii) Montgomery College is one of the colleges of the North Harris Montgomery Community College District, Texas.

d. British Open University (BOU) in Europe.

   i) BOU has expanded its charter as an Open University with electronic communications media.

   ii) The Open University is the most renowned institution in distance learning that proffered the first support model that is emulated by many other universities around the world.

e. Walden University, Minnesota.

3. **CONSORTIA/COLLABORATION OF EDUCATIONAL INSTITUTIONS.** A third model that is emerging is a virtual institution created through the collaboration of several educational institutions. These institutions are sharing academic and network resources, expertise, and providing their academic services through their collective programs. Illustrative programs are the following:

a. Western Governors' Conference: 13 Western States in the United States

b. Virginia Community College System: Electronic Learning Institute (ELI)

c. Maine Educational Network: Statewide telecourse network

d. Lionhawk

   i) Collaboration of two "Big Ten" Universities (United States)

   ii) Pennsylvania State University and Iowa State University

e. World Community College

   i) Leading community colleges providing a virtual education internationally

   ii) Partnering with CCID to provide education internationally to developing countries

f. Inter-University Cooperation Programmes (ICPs): Erasmus Programme

   i) European universities

   ii) Financed for forming ICPs to

      a) Exchange staff, faculty and/or students;

      b) Develop joint curricula; and

      c) Support visiting faculty and staff from other countries to explore the development of ICP-type consortia.

4. **CORPORATIONS PROVIDING ADMINISTRATION, MARKETING, AND/OR DELIVERY OF COURSES AND DEGREES PARTNERED WITH EDUCATIONAL INSTITUTIONS.** The fourth model combines industry and education together for the marketing, distribution, and delivery of educational programs to students with a view of "any time, any place, anywhere" as its driving theme. Illustrative virtual programs are the following:

a. College Connection of Jones Educational Cable — formerly Mind Extension University. (http://www.jec.edu/cc/map.html)

   i) This corporation delivers education from 11 colleges and universities to home and office.

   ii) College Connection's participating universities offer a

variety of Master's Degrees, Bachelor's Degree Completion Programs, Associate's Degrees, and Certificate Programs.

b. Electronic University Network. (http://www.wcc-eun.com/indes.html)

   i) A corporation that assists colleges and universities to develop, launch, and manage full degree programs, and the required courses, on their 'virtual campuses' on America Online.

   ii) The EUN now supports 10 colleges and universities with degrees online.

c. Virtual University. (http://www.euro.net/innovation/Web_Word_Base/News.Base/9410/ Virtual_University.html)

   i) This university is an incorporated, nonprofit organization that provides education to both traditional and nontraditional students who find it difficult gaining access to a conventional college or university.

   ii) Virtual Online University's goal is to provide low-cost, high quality education; offer distance learning using interactive, interdisciplinary methods outside of, or supplementing traditional learning paths; conduct research and provide electronic delivery systems.

Educators may find on the Internet a fifth model: free courses for knowledge-based learning provided through a host network corporation and participating educational providers. This model does not fit the architecture of the Virtual Education Environment of this article: accredited and degree granting.

In addition to the models described from Figure 4, there are several programs in industry and education supporting virtual, distance, and asynchronous learning environments. These are listed and diagrammed as Figure 5.

New Programs and Research for Virtual Education

The following programs provide virtual learning instructional models, infrastructure support, and research. They represent leading programs that address various components of a virtual education and provide research and potential standards for all business educators:

- Going the Distance: This is a program offered from the Public Broadcast Services (PBS) of telecourses to support distance learning.

- Asynchronous Learning Networks: This program is a Kettering Sloan-funded project for networks with communication services.

- Internet II: This is a federal program to establish a high speed Internet for the postsecondary schools.

- Megaserver and Network Environments: This project is a network

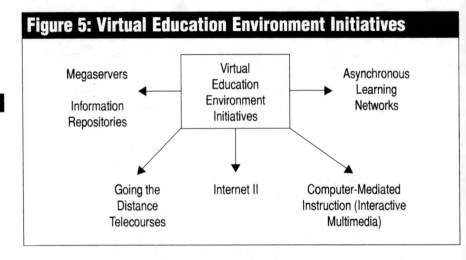

Figure 5: Virtual Education Environment Initiatives

infrastructure environment consisting of powerful megaservers for information repositories and a powerful high-speed network.

- Computer-Mediated Instruction: This type of instruction is a partnership between industry and education in the delivery of computer-mediated instruction with positive results in mathematics and writing.

Going the Distance is a national initiative, enabling students to earn their Associate degree at a distance through the medium of telecourses. *Going the Distance* commenced in August 1994 as the initial program under PBS's workforce initiative, *Ready to Earn*. More than 100 postsecondary institutions offered their courses and degree programs through 36 public television outlets in 27 states by the program's second year of implementation. Jacques DuBois is the PBS Project Director for *Going the Distance*. DuBois indicates that each college retains control over telecourses offered on *Going the Distance* and is responsible for the administration of their syllabi, course, and degree requirements. Further, he emphasizes, students in these telecourses meet the same requirements as their on-campus counterparts in regard to assignments, examinations, and grades. The postsecondary institution administers its own student admissions and registration, faculty, and university services. PBS licenses to colleges the right to each telecourse in its catalog. The colleges and universities assign a faculty member to teach each course (*Going the Distance*, 1997).

ASYNCHRONOUS LEARNING NETWORKS (ALN). ALNs are computer networks designed to reduce the isolation of home study students by giving them a means to communicate (through the network) to other students, faculty, and the administration with supporting electronic messaging systems and computer conferencing. An instructional research and development program funded by the Kettering Sloan Foundation into ALN was done over two phases with the Virginia Community College System (http://eli..nv.cc.va.us/PROG_DES.HTM). Phase I reviewed an independent study model with computer networks. Phase II replaced independent learning with a more collaborative learning environment (Lemke, 1997). ALNs are a required component of a virtual education as they provide a means for communication and interactivity for remote students such as home-bound, work site, regional, domestic, or international students.

INTERNET II. This is a proposed federal program to provide a second Internet to postsecondary institutions. This federally funded program would develop a second Internet specifically for the educational environment. Internet II is a project designed to improve Internet capabilities at over one hundred universities, colleges, laboratories, and libraries. Internet II is a national network that would be the nearly exclusive domain of the educational community. The Internet II project will also develop a new family of advanced applications to meet emerging academic requirements in research, teaching, and learning. Currently, the federal government has released a grant request document for those institutions desiring to be a part of the initial Internet II network.

MEGASERVER AND NETWORK ENVIRONMENTS: CAL POLY WITH COMPUTER MANUFACTURERS AND TELCO CORPORATIONS. California University (Cal Poly at San Luis Obispo) has created a Virtual Education Environment for the university system. This development and research project is a combined effort of partners from the university system and industry (computer manufacturers and telecommunication providers). This technical project supports ALNs and provides the description of an advanced network that utilizes megaservers and subservers over WANs and LANs using asynchronous transfer mode (ATM) telecommunication services for the provision of virtual classrooms and all network services to students on local campus and remote sites.

> The idea is to use spare capacity at the university's administration server to provide simultaneous access for all students on the university's widely spaced campuses. The students will be able to hear and see lectures, copy notes, look at slides and overheads, and similar materials. The new system is wired into student dormitories, so conferencing, e-mail, and tutorials will be available . . . at any time.

A host system (megaserver) and subservers work over ATM, which serves as a repository for large files, presentations, and video. A user calls a file from the megaserver; a subserver at San Luis Obispo holds it temporarily for quicker access. Students have advanced messaging capabilities to provide the asynchronous learning network support. This advanced network has much potential. For example, it may become one of the models that will be emulated to insure that voice, video, and data repositories are available at virtually all remote sites.

Research by the faculty is ongoing to assess the effectiveness and efficiency of this virtual learning environment and network. In addition to the implementation of this advanced network infrastructure, Cal Poly has implemented Computer-Mediated Instruction through a working, collaborative partnership with Academic Systems Corporation.

169

COMPUTER-MEDIATED INSTRUCTION. Academic Systems Corporation founded by Dr. Bernard Gifford (formerly of University of California at Berkeley and Vice President at Apple Corporation) develops computer-mediated courseware with emphases on a continuous improvement program and ongoing research with its educational partners and consumers. (See Figure 6)

Dr. Gifford and his employees are genuinely interested in enhancing the effectiveness and efficiency of instruction in higher education. This unique corporation illustrates the theory that you can partner education and industry to produce powerful results in higher education via a distributed computer-mediated instruction model. Their courseware provides students instruction (on campus and with a virtual network option) via networked, multimedia computer systems that also provide continuous online, real-time feedback during the learning processes. "It is a model that excites many proponents of instructional computing, who have been waiting for software sophisticated enough to capture students' attention, challenge them, and assess their progress (Gifford, 1997).

Dr. Gifford through his writings, presentations, and research emphasizes that this computer-mediated model works and integrates a complete model of instruction — a sound, applied pedagogical approach that is achieving results (Gifford, 1997). This learner-centered model of instruction (groups or individuals) is supported by human resources, static and dynamic instructional materials, and instructional support via distributed mediated learning technologies. The corporation does what industry does best — to develop, test, validate, support, and continually update multimedia courseware for education. Its educational partners do what education does best — to provide instruction to the students and to provide the "best in practice" teaching and instructional models. Together they form a unique collaborative environment to increase the effectiveness and efficiency of learning for all students. Their production capabilities (housed in the San Francisco Bay area) have produced some of the most engaging interactive multimedia courseware that is available on the market. Additionally, they provide an instructional management system of online reports, as well as on-site support to aid the faculty and campus experts.

Business education is experiencing widespread change with the virtual education model. The previous section illustrates the breadth of work that is being done within the United States (and abroad) to understand how to provide and support the asynchronous environment of a virtual education. Further, business educators need to know how to provide the communications and instructional support for faculty and students within the context of the mission of a university and high school. These efforts, combined with the organizational structures being implemented and the transformation of courses and degrees at hundreds of institutions, will extend the educational system. This extension — the virtual, online campus — has become an accepted mode of instruction in today's transformed information age. Today's educators need to be aware of virtual education models that provide and support an environment that brings the services of campus to remote

Figure 6: Computer-Mediated Instruction

A New Model of Computer-Mediated Instruction, Learning, and Assessment

Human Teaching and Learning Resources

Instructors	Teaching Assistants
Peer Learning Groups	Off-Campus Experts

Static and Dynamic Instructional Text

Traditional and Dynamic Test	Archived Digital Data Resources
Specialized E-Bulletin Boards	E-Mail and Virtual Chalkboards

Learners

As individuals or as members of:

Heterogeneous Groups	Heterogeneous Groups
Heterogeneous Groups	Heterogeneous Groups

Instructional Support and Distributed Mediated Learning Technologies

Real-Time Task-Specific Assessment and Feedback	Real-Time Task-Specific Assessment and Feedback	Real-Time Task-Specific Assessment and Feedback

Multimedia Authoring System and Related Utilities

Multimedia Authoring System and Related Utilities

Multimedia Authoring System and Related Utilities

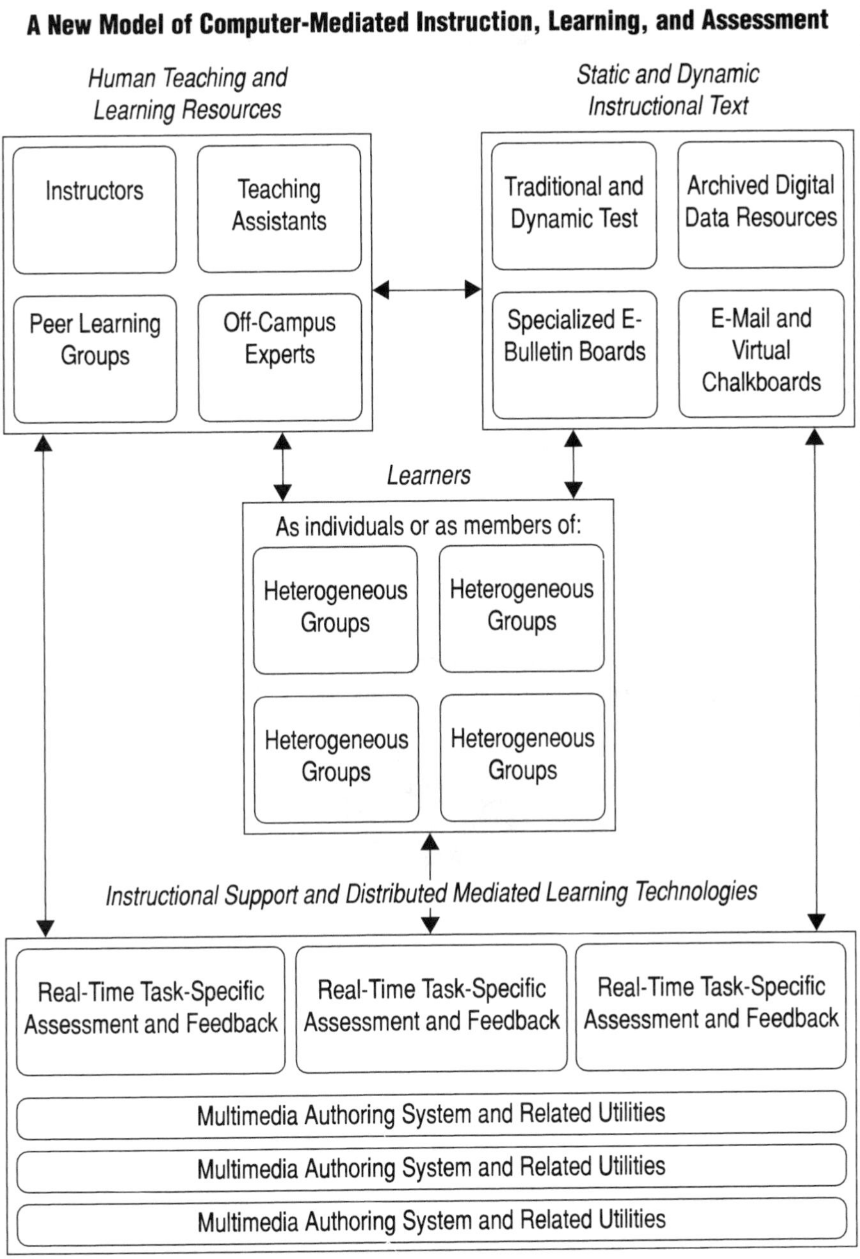

Source: Gifford, B. From Theory to Practice: The Odyssey of the Distributed Learning Model. A presentation at the American Association of Higher Education. [http://www.academic.com/research/mllibrary/aahe.asp], March 18, 1997.

students — just as well as fundamental academic content. The next section describes the support environment for a Virtual Education Environment.

Support Environment: Virtual Education Environment

The Virtual Education Environment described in this chapter mandates that an institution is to provide the support for all university functions for its remote students. Many universities and schools are successfully implementing this vital support infrastructure to meet the needs of the university, students, and faculty. Figure 7 illustrates many of the functions that these organizations provide. Thus, virtual universities have a virtual organization with a mission and charter. These Virtual Education Environment organizations provide planning, budgets, and operations across all elements of an educational organization.

As the virtual university may be an extension of current campuses, instructional support and professional development are required for the faculty and students. All faculty and students may need training and support in the use of networked systems and services to deliver and receive education in this environment. It is conceivable that many faculty may be adjunct faculty working remotely as instructors. All faculty will need the support program for this new virtual environment.

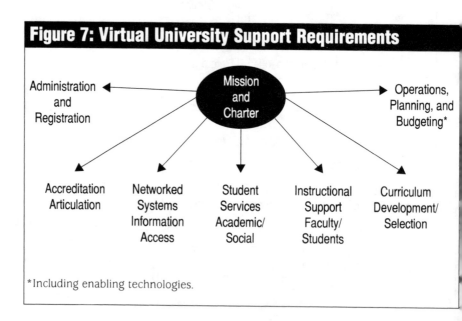

Figure 7: Virtual University Support Requirements

*Including enabling technologies.

ADMINISTRATION AND REGISTRATION. This environment provides online administration, applications, registration, fees processing, and student records. Further, marketing, public relations, online catalogs, and communications for students and faculty are required via information networks.

ACCREDITATION AND ARTICULATION. Accredited universities are extending their charter and providing their accredited programs via a virtual environment. Virtual universities that operate via voice, video, and data networks are receiving accreditation. These accreditations provide validity to the degrees offered through many distance learning technologies. Included in the list of accredited programs are virtual programs that are composed of collaborative, participating universities that have developed articulation agreements. These articulation agreements are including articulation beyond the normal boundaries and include domestic and international agreements.

173

NETWORKED SYSTEMS AND INFORMATION ACCESS. Voice, video, and data systems must be carefully planned in an Information Resource Plan. These plans for networks must provide high-speed information access to on- and off-campus servers and information repositories. Each campus and organization must carefully develop the standards and protocols they will use to collect, store, and access information. The communications and messaging enabling applications will be a part of this plan. Networking applications that support the individual and group activities are categorized as groupware. Groupware/messaging applications are requisite components of a virtual university. Figure 8 illustrates some of the groupware applications needed in a Virtual Education Environment.

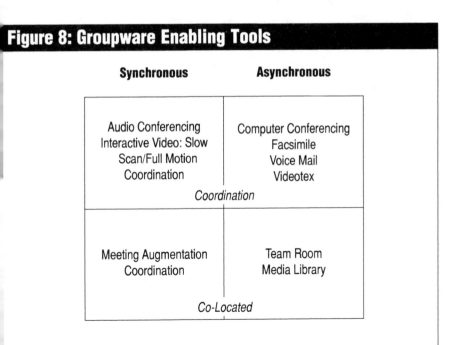

Figure 8: Groupware Enabling Tools

	Synchronous	Asynchronous
	Audio Conferencing Interactive Video: Slow Scan/Full Motion Coordination	Computer Conferencing Facsimile Voice Mail Videotex
	Coordination	
	Meeting Augmentation Coordination	Team Room Media Library
	Co-Located	

Source: Grenier, R. and Metes, G. *Enterprise Networking: Working Together Apart.* Digital Press.

STUDENT SERVICES. One of the critical functions that links the "traditional" university is the provision of a complete set of services to the "non-traditional" remote students. These range from all application processes, acquisition of books and curriculum materials, library and learning resources, veterans' services, industry internships, online newspapers, providing online messaging systems to allow participation in student organizations, and socialization options. The off-campus students should be made to feel as welcome as the on-campus students believes Dr. Maxwell King, President of the Brevard Community College system in Florida (King, 1997).

174

INSTRUCTIONAL SUPPORT FOR FACULTY AND STUDENTS. Educational institutions must provide training and professional development support for faculty and students in order for them to participate fully in the Virtual Education Environment.

1. Baseline
    a. Accessing and utilizing each network application.
    b. Accessing, downloading, and transferring information to, from, and among information sources.
    c. Providing user IDs to access on-campus systems, servers, and networks; local and Internet access.

2. Computer and Network Literacy for Instructional Support
    a. Training for computer and network access.
    b. Testing computer literacy.
    c. Providing training in computer literacy.
    d. Taking and providing courses over remote networks.

3. Common User Application Training and Support
    a. Instructing for end-user tools: word processor, spreadsheets, and presentation software.
    b. Providing instruction in communication tools: electronic mail, conferencing, and bulletin boards.
    c. Using modern electronic white boards with print capabilities.
    d. Using Internet access and browsers in a network computing environment.

4. Advanced Application Environment to Meet Course Requirements
    a. Providing support for multimedia applications.
    b. Training in the development of compound document environment, hypertext links and/or Web-based repositories, and audio and video systems.

5. Synchronous and Asynchronous Learning Environments.
    a. Understanding the models for networked individual and team-work: same time/same place or different time/different place.

  b. Developing instruction for co-located and/or distributed learning environments.

 6. Instructional Management Systems

  a. Assessing real-time and online evaluation with new evaluation systems.

   i) Pre- and post-testing.

   ii) Formative assessments and summative assessments.

  b. Providing online reporting systems.

 7. Access to Support Personnel

  a. Provisioning students with: faculty, teaching assistants, student mentors, content experts, tutors, bulletin boards, and discussion groups.

  b. Scheduling faculty: content and instructional experts, instructional materials development and dissemination, ListServs, and USENETS across networks.

  c. Providing virtual learning organizational support personnel.

CURRICULUM DEVELOPMENT/SELECTION. The Virtual Education Environment provides knowledge transfer — as does the traditional university. The delivery medium expands beyond the delivery by a faculty member to delivery via recorded voice, text, graphics, image, and video. The instructional materials need to be developed for a Virtual Education Environment. Faculty will be selecting multimedia materials and/or developing materials to support their academic areas. Institutions are providing distance learning support organizations to assist faculty; for example, this is occurring at the Distance Learning Center at the University of Missouri.

OPERATIONS, PLANNING, AND BUDGETING. Our schools and colleges are all approaching the Virtual Education Environment through the establishment of planning documents, budgets, and operational procedures to include instructional and network technology. The approach may be one or more of the following:

- Establishment of centralized, separate virtual/distance learning organization.
- Integration of distance learning within each academic unit.
- Contract services for distance learning.

Enabling Technologies for a Virtual Education Environment

One of the drivers of the change toward the Virtual Education Environment is advancing technology. There are several critical technologies from the current and coming base of the Virtual Education Environment. "Inter-organizational systems, groupware, document-based processing, information refineries, executive support systems, and other information technologies have a fundamental impact on coordination and control" (Hald and Konsynski in Bradley, Hausman, and Nolan 1993). These technologies are displayed in Figure 9. Business educators are often responsible for providing computer literacy and application programs. Often, this responsibility alone is daunting. However, we must move beyond a support-only stance to planning the inclusion of all the

176

following technologies and networks into our programs for instructional efficiency and effectiveness for this emerging Virtual Education Environment. The new standards developed for business education will require the operations, planning, and budgeting of these systems into our curricula. Hald and Konsynski (1993) outlined several important technology trends that are accelerating an organizational shift to high information intensity. Outlined below are the components that will be needed for the virtual environment as schools become more information-based and information becomes available on demand.

Figure 9: Enabling Technologies

Enabling Technologies for a Virtual Education Environment

1. Megaservers, Information Warehouses

2. Multimedia and/or Interactive Media

3. Software Integrated Circuits and Codification

4. Reliable Optical Scanning Character Recognition

5. Bulk Pricing Information Database and Network Purchases

6. Inexpensive, High-Capacity Distribution Channels

7. Automated Indexing and Routing Technology

8. Information in Electronic Form

9. Hypertext and Hypermedia

10. Document/Data Formats and Automated Recognition

Source: Hald and Konsynski in Bradley, Hausman, and Nolan. Bradley, S., Hausman, J. A., and Nolan, R. L. (1993). *Globalization, Technology and Competition: The Fusion of Computers and Telecommunications in the 1990s.* Boston: Harvard Business School Press.

- **INFORMATION SERVERS: MEGASERVERS.** These are high performance servers that will provide the repository for archived digital data resources. Reduced instruction-set computers and multiprocessing techniques will deliver information requests to end-users at tremendous speeds. These repositories will be able to distribute holdings to users expediently.

177

- **MULTIMEDIA/INTERACTIVE MEDIA.** Powerful courseware that takes advantage of learning style and media composition to the learners' advantage.

- **SOFTWARE INTEGRATED CIRCUITS AND KNOWLEDGE CODIFICATION.** With object-oriented programming, developers and users of information resources can "encapsulate" knowledge and software functions in modules combined with other modules like integrated circuits.

- **HIGH-CAPACITY AND HIGH-RELIABILITY OPTICAL SCANNING AND CHARACTER RECOGNITION.** Institutions and libraries will utilize electronic information sources for capturing research or printed materials with powerful scanners. The captured information will be made available via indexed electronic online networked libraries.

- **BULK PRICING OF CORPORATE INFORMATION PURCHASES.** Educational systems or multi-state consortiums will ask for bulk pricing through united purchase programs to reduce the acquisition costs.

- **INEXPENSIVE AND HIGH-CAPACITY DISTRIBUTION CHANNELS.** The advent of Internet II will provide an inexpensive "private network" for the university environment — much like private, high speed networks for corporations.

- **AUTOMATED INDEXING AND ROUTING TECHNIQUES.** Just as in automated records management systems, vendors of information will soon deploy artificial intelligence-based systems to index and route "real-time" textual and compound documents.

- **HYPERTEXT AND HYPERMEDIA.** Hypertext is the dynamic linking of parts of different documents to one another based upon related content or supporting resources. Education was the first organization to exploit hypertext within documents.

- **AVAILABILITY OF EXTERNAL AND INTERNAL INFORMATION IN ELECTRONIC FORM.** The reliance on a networked computing environment will mandate academic support systems available in electronic form. Digital authorization certificates will provide access programs for institutions.

- **DOCUMENT FORMAT STANDARDS AND AUTOMATED RECOGNITION.** Internal standards organizations have developed standards for the markup of technical documents (SGML), and a markup language has been developed for hypertext support for documents on servers

(HTML). Scanners have been developed that will insert the markup language into existing documents.

Summary

The Virtual Education Environment is a complex new structure that business education and all academic disciplines will be charged to provide. As business educators address the new standards for business students, a clear mandate has provided the direction to support students in a traditional education and a Virtual Education Environment.

This charge is mandated to "Select and apply the tools of technology as they relate to personal and business decision-making" (*National Standards for Business Education*, p. 3). Further, our standards clearly illustrate the importance of these technologies as a part of the basic core of knowledge required of students to enter the field of business. What better way to illustrate this importance than to incorporate the use of advanced technologies in the provisioning of the student's education?

> *The ability to use computers efficiently with other components of information systems, a basic area of business education, is also a 'must' for everyone in our increasingly technological society. One of the most important components of business education is information systems. In this critical area students learn to use computers as tools in conjunction with related software. In addition, they learn to make decisions, to produce professional documents, to communicate via Internet, and to research topics utilizing libraries around the world* (*National Standards for Business Education*, p. 4).

Our leaders foresaw the advent of a Virtual Education Environment—we must meet the challenge.   The field of information systems is critical to business education throughout all educational levels. Name changes that reflect information systems curricula, such as Office Administration becoming Administrative Information Systems, become more prevalent. Also, the restructuring of our universities to meet fiscal requirements forces our administrators to provide an extended learning environment for students throughout a broader geographic spectrum. Business educators are challenged with an "awesome" responsibility: provide the educational knowledge and technology infrastructure to expand our field (and others) with the application of technology for a Virtual Education Environment.

The natural expansion of our field with technology provides one of the most exciting changes that brings business education to the forefront of education: leadership in the application and use of technology to expand education to all students — any time, any place, and anywhere.

Finally, the Virtual Education Environment is a structure with a set of electronic enabling tools to help our students and faculties meet the instructional goals via this new structure. The most important component of this emerging structure is people: faculty providing and facilitating instruction to students (regardless of time and place). Business educators, the time is now to seize this wonderful opportunity with our natural talents. As Grenier and Metes stated:

> The key is people—capable and empowered to do their jobs through access to information, when and where they need it. We must design work processes that optimize the ability we have to move information throughout our extended enterprise. We need to communicate these concepts to our people, train them so that they will be comfortable with these tools, and demonstrate our action and reward. We need to energize our organization to be flexible, innovative and capable (Grenier and Metes, 1992).

179

Resources

Resources for business educators to use as they restructure their programs and curricula for this Virtual Educational Environment are included in Tables 1, 2, and 3. These tables provide listings of programs related to Virtual Education Environments including professional associations. Only 10 from each category are listed to demonstrate the prolific interest in virtual education.

Table 1: Beyond the Internet

Virtual Education Environment References

(Note: this listing is limited to one page for the Yearbook. Contact the author at hwalker@mainline.com for more complete listings)

http://alpha.lansing.cc.mi.us/~marygarrett/cte/july24.htm	Virtual Colleges by Chuck Bettison. Cause Professional Paper Series #14. Some examples of virtual colleges.
http://eli.nv.cc.va.us/PROG_DES.HTM	Extended Learning Institution
http://homepage.interaccess.com/~ghoyle/	Descriptions of distance education Web sites, along with hot links. Resources chosen for their quality and reputation.
http://hpcnet.soton.ac.uk/vc/submit.html	Submit a Course to Virtual Classroom
http://jrbnt.vuse.vanderbilt.edu/alnpaper/virtualuniv.htm	"Virtual Universities: Wave of the Future Using Past Technology"
http://microsoft.com/education/hed/action.htm#calculus	The Calculus Consortium Project: Technology in Math Education
http://tecfa.unige.ch/edu-comp/WWW-VL/edu-page.html	Education on the Internet: Maintained Collection of Pointers 1 Education on the Net — Indexes 2 Distance Education 3 Education Subjects on the Net 4 Resources for Teachers 5 WWW and Gopher Reference Pages for education 6 Education Journals 7 Reference 8 Mailing Lists
http://webster.commnet.edu/hp/pages/darling/journals.htm	Journals and Newsletters for Distance Education
http://webster.commnet.edu/hp/pages/darling/distance.htm	Resources for Distance Education. A list maintained by Dr. Charles Darling, Capital Community-Technical College, Hartford, CT
http://whodunit.uchicago.edu/i2/he1101.htm	The Chronicle of Higher Education, November 1, 1996. "Administration Plans the Next Generation of Campus Networks" Re: Internet II — Campus Web backbone
http://www.academic.com/news/chronicl.asp	The Chronicle of Higher Education. "Mediated Learning." Academic Systems Corporation.
http://www.aetn.org/education/distance.html	Going the Distance: First national initiative to earn an Associates of Arts degree at a distance. AETN joins the initiative.

Table 2: Virtual Universities

Open University of British Columbia	CyberEd. University of Massachusetts at Dartmouth
University Online	Electronic University Network
Home Education Network	Edmond's Center for Continuing Education
CNU Online. Christopher Newport University	New School for Social Research
Edroads City University	ME/U Education Services Center
Foothill Global Access	New Hampshire College
Mercy College	California College for Health Sciences
Eastern Oregon State College	Pitt Community College Distance Learning
Diversity University, Inc.	University of Florida, DOCE
Walden University	Columbia Pacific University
Australian Correspondence Schools	Tele-universite de l'Universite du Quebec
Virtual Online University	Gymnasia Virtualis
Mentys—The Internet Computer Institute	Space.edu
Altos Education Network	CALnetwork
Spectrum	Free Academy of Career Training
@LearnSkills	ZD Net University
Microsoft Online Institute	Seattle Central Community College
Laramie County Community College	University College of the Fraser Valley
URA Educators	Online Education Limited
Flex Learning Systems	OnLine Campus University of Phoenix
Portland Community College Open Campus	The Open University of the UK
Athabasca University	Virtual Online University
The Fielding Institute	The Graduate School of America
Design for Leadership (Defiance College)	Miami Christian University
Online Bible Institute	University of Berkeley
Barrington University	Language Connect University
The Virtual Art School	Writers on the Net

181

Table 3: Virtual Education Environment

Associations, USENETS, and Listservs

ASSOCIATIONS	
ADEC Distance Learning Consortium	http://www.ces.ncsu.edu/adec/
American Center for the Study of Distance Education	http://www.cde.psu.edu/DE/default.html
British Association for Open Learning	
Education Commission of the States	http://www.ecs.org/
Institute for Academic Technology	http://www.iat.unc.edu
Institute for Distance Education	http://www.umuc.edu/ide/ide.html
International Council for Distance Education	http://www.icde.org/icde/
International University Consortium	
Journal on Computer-Mediated Instruction	http://www.usc.edu/dept/annenberg/oscfp.html
SmartStates Virtual University	http://www.concerto.com/smart/vu/vu.html
South Bay Advanced Educational Technology Consortium. (ADTECH)	
Southeastern Pennsylvania Consortium for Information Technology and Training	
Southwest Center for Advanced Technological Study	
The Commonwealth of Learning	http://www.col.org
U.S. Department of Education	Gopher://gopher.ed.gov
U.S. Distance Learning Association	http://www.usdla.org
Western Brokering Project	http://www.wiche.edu/broker/bppage.htm
Western Cooperative for Educational Telecommunications	http://www.wiche.edu/telecom/techresor.htm
Western Governors' Association and Western Interstate Commission for Higher Education (WICHE)	http://www.wiche.edu

NEWSGROUPS
alt-education-distance-FAQ — Dr. E's Eclectic Compendium of Electronic Resources for Adult/Distance Education
alt.education.distance
alt.education.alternative
Gopher:alt.education.distance
Misc.education
misc.education.adu.lt

LISTSERVS
Gopher:UKCC.uky.edu
AEDNET

References

Bradley, S., Hausman, J. A., and Nolan, R. L. (1993). *Globalization, Technology, and Competition: The Fusion of Computers and Telecommunications in the 1990s*. Boston: Harvard Business School Press.

Brevard Community College. (1997, April, 13 and 1996, December 4). Telephone interviews with Cocoa Campus President and Hazel R. Walker, University of South Carolina.

Brevard Community College. (1997, October). [Online]. Available: http://www.brevard.cc.fl.us.

DeLoughry, T. J. (1997, October 25). Computerized Courses Change the Way Mathematics Is Taught. *Chronicle of Higher Education: Academic NET*. [Online]. Available: http://www.academic.com/news/chronicl.asp.

Distance Learning Design Center for the University of Missouri-Columbia. (1997). [Online]. Available: http://www.missouri.edu/ ~ dldcww/index.htm.

Educational Commission of the States. (1997). [Online]. Available: http://www.ecs.org.

Electronic University Network. (1997). [Online]. Available: http://www.wcc-eun.com/index.html.

Gifford, B. (1997, March 18). *From Theory to Practice: The Odyssey of the Distributed Learning Model*. A presentation at the American Association of Higher Education. [Online]. Available: http://www.academic.com/research/mllibrary/aahe.asp.

Going the Distance. (1997). [Online]. Available: http://www.brevard.cc.fl.us/distlrn/adx.html.

Gorbachev, M. (1986). In a speech to the 28th Congress of the Soviet Communist Party.

Grenier, R. and Metes, G. (1992). Enterprise Networking: Working Together Apart. *Digital Press*. [Online]. Available: http://www.wcc-eun.com/bcc/index.html.

Hutchinson, C. (1996, April). Snares in the Charmed Circle. *Times Higher Education Supplement*.

IBM Global Campus Helps Higher Education Transform Teaching and Learning Through Computer Networks. [Online]. Available: http://www.hied.ibm.com/igc/press.html.

Internet II. (1997). [Online]. Available: http://www.scout.cs.wisc.edu/scout/notes/ref/in2general.html.

JEC College Connection. (1997). [Online]. Available: http://www.jec.edu/cc/map.html.

King, M. C. (1997). Welcome From the President. Brevard Community College. [Online]. Available: http://www.brevard.cc.fl.us.

King, M. C., Koller, A., and Eskow, S. (1997). *World Community College: Using Technology to Provide Interactive, Comprehensive, Personal Learning*. [Online]. Available: http://www.brevard.cc.fl.us/distlrn/wcc-arti.html.

Lemke, R. A. (1997). *Electronic Learning Institute*. [Online]. Available: http://eli.nv.cc.va.us/PROG_DES.HTM.

National Business Education Association. (1995). *National Standards for Business Education: What America's Students Should Know and Be Able to Do in Business*. Reston, VA: National Business Education Association.

The Report of Task Force on Distance Learning. (1992, November). [Online]. Available: http://www.cde.psu.edu/de/DE_TF.html.

Virtual Online University. (1994). [Online]. Available: http://www.euro.net/innovation/Web_Word_Base/News.Base/9410/Virtual_University.html.

Western Governors' Association. (1996, April). [Online]. Available: http://www.concerto.com/smart/vu/vunews.html.

Where's the Money for Internet II? (1997). *Education Link*. [Online]. Available: http://www.boardwatch.com/mag/97/jan/bwm.htm.